Three Years in Bloom

A Garden-Keeper's Journal

Introduction and text by Ann Lovejoy

Sasquatch Books
Seattle

Three Years in Bloom: A Garden-Keeper's Journal

Printed in Canada

ISBN 0-912365-17-X

Excerpts from *The Year In Bloom: Gardening for All Seasons in the Pacific Northwest* by Ann Lovejoy © Sasquatch Books 1987

Cover art by Jean Emmons

Interior illustrations by Louise Smith

Design by Weekly Typography & Graphic Design
Designers: Frances Porter Milner, Yoshiko Tsuji, and Jane Rady
Seattle, Washington

Typeset in Caslon and Fenice

Printed in Canada

Sasquatch Books
1931 Second Avenue
Seattle, Washington 98101
(206) 441-5555

Also by Sasquatch Books
Northwest Best Places
Seattle Best Places
Seattle Cheap Eats
Cooking with Eight Items or Less
The Year in Bloom
The Fall of the House of WPPSS
Washingtonians

All gardeners have a perfect garden of the inner eye. While we may know in our hearts that such visions are rarely achievable, the pursuit of our vision provides satisfactions that the strictly pragmatic can't imagine. To make a garden, on any scale at all, is to create an environment, a world of one's own. To be in the garden, absorbed in such creative efforts, is to be deeply content. The garden may not ever be finished, and will certainly never be perfect. That is as it should be; the point is not mastery, but cooperation. When gardeners give plants their intelligent attention, the results are bound to be wonderful. Could there be any better reward for our thought, our planning, our experiments, and our labors, than an entire year in bloom?

Ann Lovejoy, *The Year in Bloom*

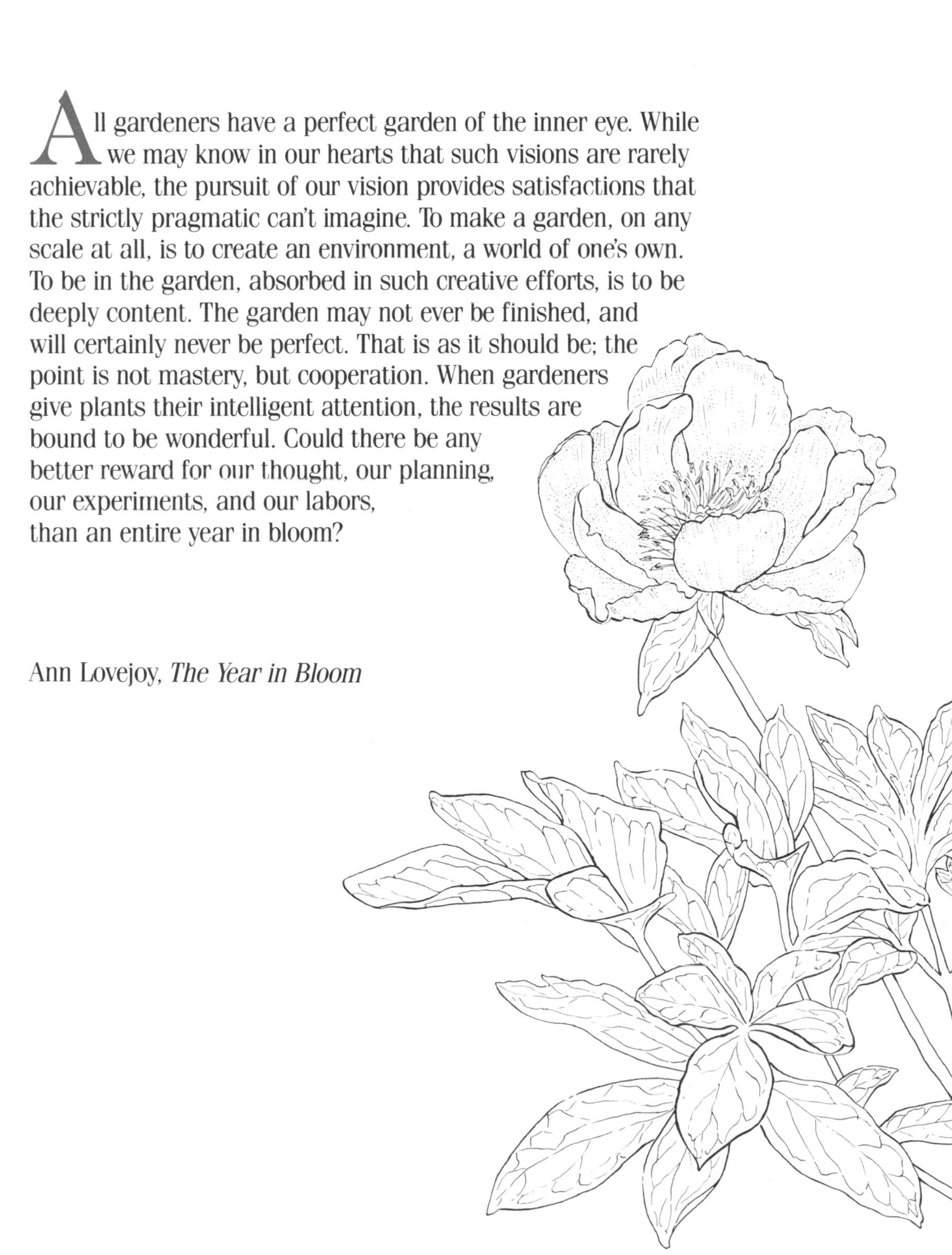

INTRODUCTION

When the idea of garden record-keeping is brought up, most gardeners respond with impatience. Why add to the already innumerable garden chores? Why add something that takes time which would otherwise be spent in the garden itself? It seems like too much trouble, and for what?

The rewards may not be intuitively obvious, yet there are many for those who will trouble themselves with such details. What's more, the penalties of *not* keeping records are equally numerous and equally certain to visit the hapless gardener who neglects this unromantic chore. Every dedicated, experienced gardener comes to it sooner or later. Even the simplest, most primitive records can keep your successes fresh, help you avoid repeating the worst mistakes, and assist in the sometimes confusing process of learning the specific qualities and microclimates of your own garden.

The best reason for record-keeping is simple human nature: despite our best intentions, we forget. When spring rains softly on the soil, who remembers that August bakes a particular area to a crackling crisp? Had a minute been taken last summer to scribble down a note to one's future self, the forewarned gardener would now be amending the soil well, adding peat, manure, and builders' sand, before tucking in the bedding plants (which instead are, alas, once again doomed to fry). When we sow all those pans of seed in late winter, we smile at the thought that, when they emerge, we might not know which was which. Absurd! After raising a batch of rare seedlings, nursing them through their first precarious months, then seeing them off to a good start in the garden proper, it seems impossible that we will not forever know what they are or where they came from. Sad as it is, we do forget, and often quickly.

Not a few gardens are filled with plants about which their proud owners know little, a situation that makes intelligent care and companion planting difficult, to say the least. How disappointing it is to visit a garden, admire a plant, and have your eager inquiries greeted with, "Isn't that pretty? I wish I knew what it was!" The situation is further complicated by the fact that many plants are dormant, and more or less invisible, during varying times of the year. When we plan a brilliant fall display based on white autumn crocus, which are to appear dramatically through a silvery veil of creeping *Helichrysum microphyllum* in front of a group of *Heuchera* 'Purple Palace', we don't for a minute believe that six months later, seeing a blank spot, we will be forking those incredibly expensive *Colchicum autumnale* 'Album' through the heart as we absent-mindedly start to stick in a few pink verbenas. Who has never sliced a promising fat shoot of a beloved but dormant peony while planting out bulbs in late fall?

The only solution to such traumas as these is to keep careful records, using garden maps and diagrams, much as the gas and electric companies do, to keep track and ensure the continuing presence of things both seen and unseen.

One of the most significant rewards will be obvious to anybody who has ever loved and lost an unusual plant for which the name tag was misplaced. This is how we all learn to appreciate the value of naming names, and why botanical Latin has value. If you can't name it, you can only replace it if you are very, very lucky. Go to any nursery you like and start talking about this neat plant that you are pretty sure you remember buying there two years ago. Explain how it had, you know, green leaves with a toothed edge, and it wasn't very tall (though not tiny or anything) and had these sort of round blue flowers, only there was just a little white in the center. Then ask if they have any more. Go on, I dare you.

It's even worse when you half remember the cultivar name (naturally, it will be something too mortifying to say out loud, like 'Gidget's Yumyum'), yet you can't quite recall the generic name, and certainly don't know the species. Do you realize how many different kinds of plants have cultivars called 'Rose Queen'? Even when you know perfectly well what it was—a pansy, say, or a fuchsia, an iris, or a daylily—there may be thousands of named cultivars, and trying to track down a particular one by color only is almost hopeless. No matter how pleasant and helpful the nursery staff, even one such encounter is likely to drive the most hard-core to taking notes (and finding a new nursery out of sheer embarrassment).

Here, in a nutshell, is the beauty of a garden record book: had you kept records, you could look the thing up in a minute and find that it was *Geranium wallichianum* 'Buxton's Blue', which you bought at Wells Medina Nursery in 1987 for $1.98. Flip a few more pages, and you will be reminded that you planted it in the west border at the foot of your Madonna lilies, where it bloomed for six months straight until a dog excavated it along with the neighboring peony. For those who do better with visual cues, planting diagrams can be the best aid to memory, and will be especially useful where several members of a family share the same bed. Even those with no artistic pretensions can make rough sketches on graph paper. Whenever new plants are introduced, indicate their positions with a simple bubble diagram or series of circles, jotting the names inside each. (Mark the border edge and any permanent things like shrubs with a pen, but use pencil for everything else. At worst, it can always be erased, and at best, those circles will expand each year.) When you find you want a dozen more of that early white iris, take the book into the garden and you will see at once that the plant in question—that one closest to the garage—is 'White Lightning'.

Keeping close tabs on where you bought what, how much you paid, and how the plants fared is not intended to be an exercise in accounting. The point is not to total up expenditures (indeed, this is to be avoided whenever possible), but to create and maintain a personal reference source. It is fatally easy to be seduced by glossy catalogs, and only too late do you recall mournfully that, while those bulbs from Company X are cheap, vigorous, and long-lasting, those from Company Q are only cheaper. Your records may show that the mail-order plants you tucked into four-inch pots recovered from their journey quickly, and even now, two years later, are still outperforming those set directly in the ground upon arrival. After a few years similar patterns emerge, and it becomes clear that plants from a certain nursery always acclimate quickly, while another place is so far north that they send things too late. This company makes unacceptable substitutions, while that one sends along so many freebies that your order is almost doubled. Without a written record, even such important details as these tend to fade away with time.

In a sense, such record-keeping is writing your own garden book, one specific to your site, your interests, your needs. As your garden—and your gardening skill—matures, that you know the exact succession of bloom over a period of years becomes invaluable. There is no better way to orchestrate reliable border groupings and effects, for as your information builds, you will be able to scan the results of several years at a time for any given week. In time, it becomes obvious which overlappings and coincidences are consistent and which are too fickle to trust with a prominent role.

Only your own notes can tell you which annuals reliably self-sow, which early bulbs coincide in bloom each year, what spring flowers linger too long and mar the building effect of the summer border (often an entirely different color scheme). Lots of books have charts about such things, but not one of them is for *your* yard. When you're planting bulbs in fall, the notes you took in late winter will remind you where the blue reticulated iris should go; those from early spring will determine how you group the species tulips; and a review of late spring's will stop you from putting all those crimson De Caen anemones too near the soft pink polyanthus rose, 'The Fairy', again.

Throughout this book are pages for photographs. No matter how good your notes, a picture will often jog your memory best. Black-and-white shots are the most useful in terms of assessing the overall character, proportions, and backbone of any garden, but color shots are best for capturing the outstanding combinations, whether triumphs or total failures. It may seem a bit silly to be taking pictures in midwinter, yet that is when the relative strength or weakness of the overall design is most apparent. If the garden is brand-new, or even if there's nothing to see in winter, take a snapshot anyway, then apply your keen mind to the problem of building a border that will be attractive and visually satisfying at any season. As your efforts pay off, those early pictures will emphasize your progress dramatically.

Some of the most gratifying pictures I have are "before and after" shots of this sort. In the first, a cracked and tilted driveway leads to a mud hole filled with blackberries and a thicket of laurel. A year later, the area is stripped clean, strongly delineated with steps and paths of old brick, and raised beds are full of fluffy soil and thriving young plants. Two years after that, vines cover the walls, the shrubs have achieved enough bulk to be impressive, and the whole has reached that happiest of states, youthful maturity.

Reminders of past successes are especially useful when starting fresh in a new location. They help to balance the natural impatience and frustration one feels when, despite a good deal of thought and work, nothing seems to be happening. A review of sequential shots of other gardens, other beds, will calm that fevered urge to get results. The gardener can relax, secure in the knowledge that it does, indeed, take three years to see how a border will shape, five years for it to fill in, seven years before it looks established and mature. For the involved gardener, these are not lost or painful years to be rushed through without pleasure, but rather years to be savored, just as one savors and delights in the infancy and toddler days of one's children.

Another crucial element to any record-keeping book is the wish list. This is where you write the names of plants you have fallen in love with, perhaps seen on a garden tour, at a slide lecture, or in a picture book. Although it is inconceivable at the time of the infatuation, time can cloud the best memory, and all too soon other plants, other places intrude. Was it the creamy early peony 'Moonrise' or the subtle 'Rushlight' that took your breath away? When catalog time rolls around, those with their wish lists in order are in the catbird seat. There is another plus to this idea; by writing these things down as they occur, you have a handy little source of suggestions when somebody says, "I wish I knew what to get you for your birthday."

Perhaps the best reward of record-keeping is the way your book can bring back summer in the border, even as you sit in front of the fire, culling through the catalogs. While you flip through the pages, making long lists, plans, and sketches, your own garden book will be your best guide. Double-check plants you are drawn to. Was that on my wish list? Didn't I already get this one? Where on earth did I put it? When you plan improvements to the border, your written comments will make clear what needs to be done. ("Find something red, low, and long-blooming for in front of the Lyme grass along the driveway.") *Alonsoa warscewiczii* 'Compacta' catches your eye in the Thompson & Morgan catalog? (Don't worry, you don't ever have to pronounce it.) It's easy to grow from seed, and blooms from midsummer into early winter. Color, size, and habit are right, a packet of seed costs less than a dollar—perfect!

In my own experience, filling a tiny urban garden with texture, color, and bloom all year round would have been far more difficult without the practical aid of a garden record book. Having to leave that garden, just as it was achieving our hopes for it, was very hard. Had I not kept that record book, it would have been harder still, for in those pages were many triumphs and many lessons learned that would certainly have been lost and forgotten but for being written down. With that book in my hand, that garden, and all it taught me, is still mine.

Now we are engaged in making another garden, larger and far more complicated. That battered old notebook is in constant use, and a new one well begun. The first few seasons are filled with observations about the existing plants, the soil, the light, and ideas for ways to fit our kind of garden comfortably around a charming, aging farmhouse. As we recovered from the move, regained energy, and grew to know the place, we began to dig, and new plants were indicated on the pages. Now, almost a year later, the garden is beginning to grow. Already, the early records of this process seem nostalgic as the present obscures the past. Our thoughts, ideas, and experiments, the successes, happy accidents, and mistakes, are covering pages as fast as we can record them—and tumbling off those same pages as fast as we can act on them. Someday, almost before we know it, this garden, too, will be bringing us whole years in bloom.

Ann Lovejoy

Ann Lovejoy
Bainbridge Island, Washington

Sample journal pages.

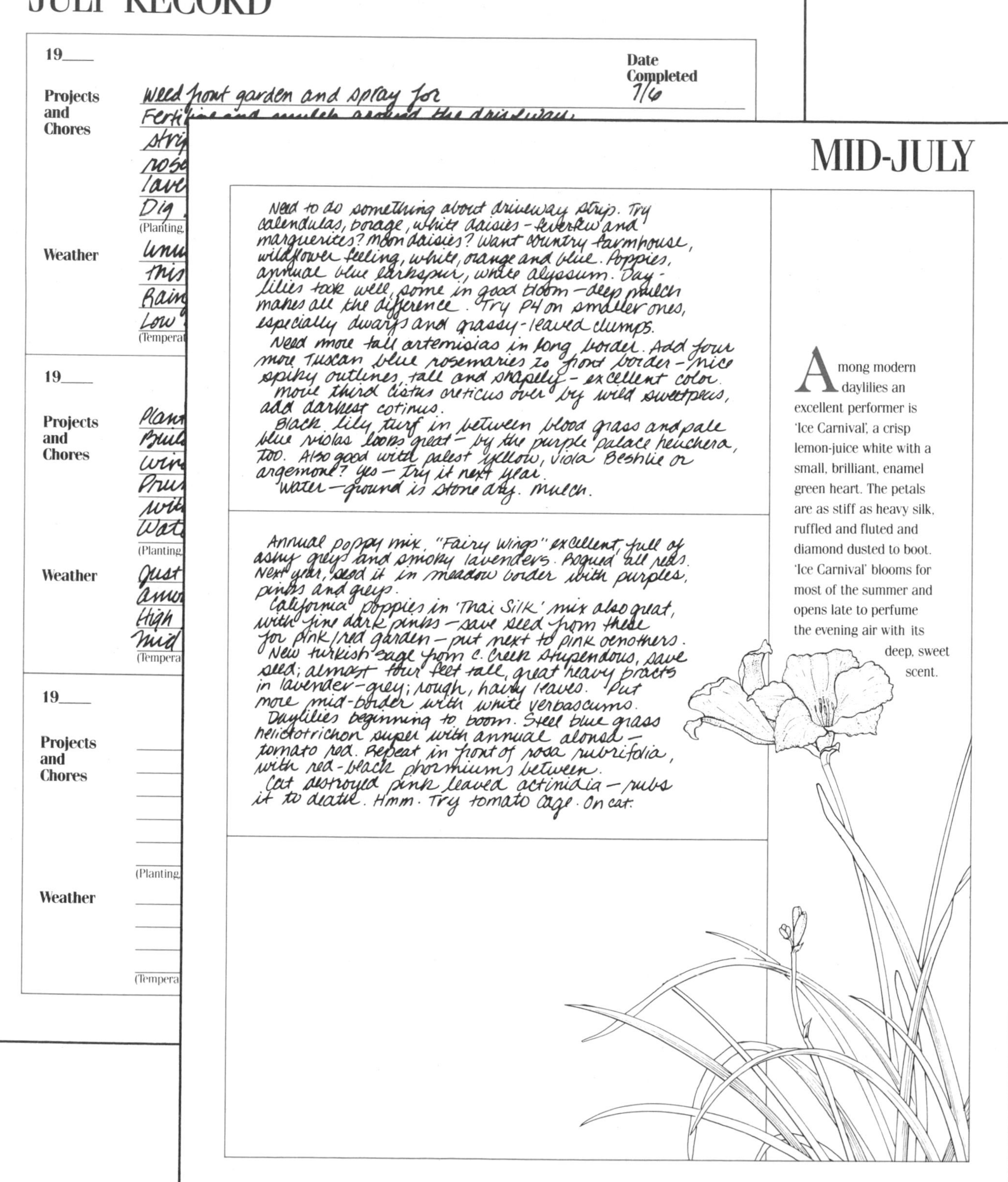

JULY RECORD

19____

Projects and Chores — Weed front garden and spray for / Fertilize and mulch around the driveway, / strip ... / rose ... / lave... / Dig ... — Date Completed 7/6

(Planting, ...

Weather — Unu... / This ... / Rain ... / Low ...

(Tempera...

19____

Projects and Chores — Plant... / Build... / Wir... / Prun... / wit... / Wat...

(Planting, ...

Weather — Just ... / amo... / High ... / Mid ...

(Tempera...

19____

Projects and Chores

(Planting, ...

Weather

(Tempera...

MID-JULY

Need to do something about driveway strip. Try calendulas, borage, white daisies – feverfew and marguerites? Moon daisies? Want country farmhouse, wildflower feeling, white, orange and blue. Poppies, annual blue larkspur, white alyssum. Daylilies took well, some in good bloom – deep mulch makes all the difference. Try P4 on smaller ones, especially dwarfs and grassy-leaved clumps.
Need more tall artemisias in long border. Add four more Tuscan blue rosemaries to front border – nice spiky outlines, tall and shapely – excellent color.
Move third Cistus creticus over by wild sweetpeas, add darkest cotinus.
Black lily turf in between blood grass and pale blue violas looks great – by the purple palace heuchera, too. Also good with palest yellow, Viola Beshlie or argemone? Yes – try it next year.
Water – ground is stone dry. Mulch.

Annual poppy mix, "Fairy Wings" excellent, full of ashy greys and smoky lavenders. Rogued all reds. Next year, seed it in meadow border with purples, pinks and greys.
California poppies in 'Thai Silk' mix also great, with fine dark pinks – save seed from these for pink/red garden – put next to pink oenothers.
New turkish sage from C. Creek stupendous, save seed; almost four feet tall, great heavy bracts in lavender-grey; rough, hairy leaves. Put more mid-border with white verbascums.
Daylilies beginning to boom. Steel blue grass helictotrichon super with annual alonsoa – tomato red. Repeat in front of rosa rubrifolia, with red-black phormiums between.
Cat destroyed pink leaved actinidia – rubs it to death. Hmm. Try tomato cage. On cat.

Among modern daylilies an excellent performer is 'Ice Carnival', a crisp lemon-juice white with a small, brilliant, enamel green heart. The petals are as stiff as heavy silk, ruffled and fluted and diamond dusted to boot. 'Ice Carnival' blooms for most of the summer and opens late to perfume the evening air with its deep, sweet scent.

Rosa 'Dainty Bess'

JANUARY RECORD

19*94*

Date Completed

Projects and Chores

Prune fruit trees and decid shrubs 1/8
Spray Peach for curl, apples for mildew + roses 1/12
Get manure for vegetable garden 1/13
Prune old raspberry canes 1/11
Do vegie garden soil tests ① potato 1/21
Transplanted Osteospurmum to 4" pots 1/9

(Planting, pruning, weeding, watering, fertilizing, pest control)

Weather

1st week weather warmer than average ½ sun, some rain

(Temperature high and low, precipitation, unusual conditions)

19*95*

Date Completed

Projects and Chores

PRUNE FRUIT TREES 1/15
CUT BACK RASPBERRIES 1/15
Spray Peach, apples* *1/17
Get manure for vegi garden
Cut off old asparagus 1/21

(Planting, pruning, weeding, watering, fertilizing, pest control)

Weather

Weather warm, rivers high + flooding mild

Warmest January on record!
Rain month of Jan ".75" thru 1/21 thru 2/1 1.73"

(Temperature high and low, precipitation, unusual conditions)

19____

Date Completed

Projects and Chores

(Planting, pruning, weeding, watering, fertilizing, pest control)

Weather

(Temperature high and low, precipitation, unusual conditions)

1994

Ordered seeds & rose bushes - need to make a veg. plan and order potatoes

Temps for 1st week days around 50° - nights at or above freezing

1995

1/15 Warm 50+ & sunny - no wind. Pulled some of the darn weeds. The winter never killed them & I'm loosing the battle. The primroses, winter jasmine, autumnalis cherry are in bloom. Some tulips are coming up. Rhubarb is growing. One peony is up. All this is worrysome - what if the cold weather comes back? All the roses are sprouting.

19____

If January seems early for planning, think again. Many a garden is doomed to failure precisely because it was the hasty product of the first warm weekend in May. Such installations are seldom thought out ahead, and usually show it sooner or later. It's so much more fun to enjoy the bounty of a thoughtfully planned garden than to struggle grimly with a haphazard one. This is an excellent time to be mulling over the possibilities, estimating your wants and needs, planning the location of each plant according to its particular demands.

One of the best things about roses is the excuse they give to play in the mud. A fine day during a January thaw is the best of all possible times to go out and fork up another patch of the iris bed, root out all (hah!) the witch grass, and dig a nice big hole.

19 94

Flower bed south side of sun room needs help! Small (under 3') evergreens of some kind to give it some vegetation in the winter. See plan (end of Jan)

Plant Elephant Garlic - done 1/18
Seeds arrived (Parks & Territorial Seed)
Weather 2nd week very mild - highs 56° Thurs 50's rest of week - lows 40's - showers 2 nights

19 95 1/21 Seeds arrived from Burpee (1/20)
Today was another spring-like day - frost this morning, but by 11:30 it was warm & sunny with no wind. Estimated temp 52°-53° - can't say for sure - I was busy outside. Cut back asparagus, phlox, topped tall canes back on roses, trimmed (wow) east side of ceanothus. Had a burn pile over 6' tall.

19____

A rare fall of snow lies on the ground and the early morning garden is hushed and still. This is the time to go exploring, when cat and bird trails are the only markings on the fresh white carpet. All below is fresh and lively green, the flower buds still plump. Creamy as ivory, flushed with rose, they are ready to open as soon as the weather relents.

LATE JANUARY

It isn't too early to renew your stock of fertilizers, check the hoses, sharpen the blades of your shovels, or oil the handles of all your tools, but that requires too much effort. We'll do that stuff in February. For now, let's content ourselves with making some sketches of the proposed pea patch, noting the locations of the trellising poles, the paths of the sun and the sprinkler. Think it all through on paper.

19 94

It rained last nite (1/21) but not enough to do much good. The months total is now .15. However the miniature iris are about 1/2" tall and some tulips are showing. Other things confused Delpheniums, lupine,

Made a small dent in weeds (left of drive)

Temps continued mild 1/22 high 56° some wind

Rain total as of 1/25 .25 inches

19 95

1/24 - Emptied finished compost pile to other side of walk + shifted/turned side 1 into side 2 + added fresh manure. Sore muscles tomorrow. Recd 3 more seed orders (Parks, Territorial, + Shepherds) Ordered Rose Restore + Vegi Restore from Burpee (15.00) Dwarf purple iris are in bloom - Seems earlier than last year - had to bait for slugs, used crushed egg shells, lost Deadline. Found pruning shears in compost pile. They are now soaking in WD40 - what a mess - it will be interesting to see if they still work.

Rain total as of 1/26 .75 in

19

Planted peas (Silroy & Precoville) 1/31. That ought to bring the winter back. (Didn't)

95

Gloriously naked and not shivering a bit, winter jasmine (*Jasminum nudiflorum*) is spangled with brilliant yellow flowers off and on throughout mild winters. The leafless branches are of a glossy, rich green that sings of spring in the quiescent winter garden. Fat with red-flushed buds, the arching wands make a wonderful tracery of color against the pale house walls. Each stem carries many flowers in succession; about an inch long, they flare from short necks into five-lobed stars. Unlike their summer cousins, they don't have that ravishing family perfume, making do with a mild, wild scent that is elusive and far from spectacular. Scent or no, for sheer cheerfulness winter jasmine can't be beat.

Jasminum nudiflorum

Vegetable Garden Plan

Corn & Potatoes on East Side of driveway – Beans in West Garden Sunflowers on west between trees & on property line. Pumpkins among flowers

(94)

- ✓ (A) Peas
- ✓ (B) Onions Foxy
- ✓ (C) Kohlrabi,
- ✓ (D) Lettuce
- ✓ (E) Peppers
- ✓ (F) Tomatoes
- ✓ (G) Squash
- ✓ (H) Carrots
- (I) ZUCCHINI
- J' Onion sets Walla Walla
- J2 Onion Walla Walla seeds
- (K) Radishes

S / E W / N

(B) Curly Parsley (F) (B)

(H) (E) (B) D Kolrabi (C)

(J') (G) (I) D (D) (A) (B) (K)

Vegi's

(95)

- (A) Peas
- (B) Carrots
- (C) Lettuce
- (D) Tomato
- (E) Squash
- (F) Zucchini
- (G) Spinach
- (H)

(G) (B) C

(D) (F) (E)

(A)

Improve this soil first!

Walla Walla Sweets Ptd 9/1

Garden South Side of Sunroom

JAN 94

Gladiolas & Sweet Peas

Ceanothus

Foxtail Lily

LOUIS IRIS

DELPHINIUM

Aster

ORIENTAL POPPY

Perennial Bachelor Button

TULIPS

FOXTAIL LILY

TULIPS

DELPH

Autumnalis Cherry

IRIS

ROSE CECIL BRUNNER

ORIENTAL POPPY

HEBE

BABYS BREATH

Archeostaphylos uva-ursi

ORIENTAL POPPY

Move any tulips & daphs in the way

convolvulus cneorum
2½ h x 3' w evergreen (silver)
white - late spring/late summer

JAN 95

Add larkspur, zinnias, & nigella curiosity and heliotrope
Modify soil for sweet peas & innoculate
See if theres a spot for white butterfly weed (asclepias)

NOTES

As winter rolls on, make some sketches, draw plans, scribble lists, and study the catalogs. While the rain pours down, mail off thosc plant and seed orders and head back to the fireside to take your ease. Come spring, the resulting flood of packages will be a treat rather than a panic-producing event.

19 94

Spread hot horse manure & wood shavings on vegie garden - all but pea area during the last week in Jan. Need to amend with nitrogen - Feb/Mar.

19 95

1/27

The wind blew from the south east Friday nite all day Saturday, Sat nite & Sunday morning about 40 mpH. Seattle had a 5.0 earthquake at 7:11 on Sat night (1/28). We didnt feel a thing.

19____

Rosemary, lavender, and oregano

FEBRUARY RECORD

19 94

Date Completed

Projects and Chores

Prune roses + move Belle Story* + Roseneef** * 2/5 2/17+18

Plant peas + onions + lettuce (or replant peas) Peas up 3/1

Start tomatoes*, Basil, French Sorrel, peppers, * 2/18

some lettuce (for sale), Heliotrope + other flowers

Plant sweet peas 2/21

Fertilized roses + rhodys + lawn 2/19

(Planting, pruning, weeding, watering, fertilizing, pest control)

Weather

See notes on next page.

Total months weather warmer than normal with less rainfall. The raingauge only showed 1/4 inch however the 'snow' came down sideways + didn't register

(Temperature high and low, precipitation, unusual conditions) I'm sure. Total more like 1/2 inch

Total Feb rain 2.0"

19 95

RASPBERRIES
FRUIT TREES
VEGI GARDEN

Date Completed

Projects and Chores

SIFT COMPOST & SPRED ON WILD FLOWER GARDEN

SPREAD MUSHROOM COMPOST

Spread rose restore + Prune roses 2/22+23

Add veg restore to onion, carrot, pea, spinach, etc areas

Fertilize grass (end of month)

Start tomato, Basil, Helio etc (late) 2/25? see March

(Planting, pruning, weeding, watering, fertilizing, pest control)

Fertilize fruit trees 1/31

Weather

(Temperature high and low, precipitation, unusual conditions)

19____

Date Completed

Projects and Chores

(Planting, pruning, weeding, watering, fertilizing, pest control)

Weather

(Temperature high and low, precipitation, unusual conditions)

19 94
Winter has returned - Cold & clear a little rain on Sunday morning (2/6) then it cleared off - cold front headed from Alaska. Figures! We have Flower & Garden Show tickets, planned to go on Thurs 2/10. Hopefully the forcasted snow & ice wont come - or at least be gone by then. 40MPH - cold winds 2/6 - 2/7. Thank heavens they blew the forcast. One very cold night (25°) or there abouts. Then back to normal 50° days 32+° nights. The only thing that seems to have suffered was the pink hardy fushia which (in its confusion) had already started to sprout. Sprouts gone now. (2/11)

19 95
Buy some creeping thyme for around apple trees - ask Sirb, good idea?
2/8 - Weather's continuing wonderful! Highs 55+ lows above freezing - Weather man is predicting cold for Sat - Wed next week. Hope hes wrong as usual - no real cold in Alaska - this would have to come from the north pole. Its been warm for so long that we mowed the lawn today - it was looking very scraggly. Everything is growing! All the tulips are coming up, even the hardy fushcia is sprouting. Peony, deutzia, etc all growing. Two of the foxtail lilies are up. Delphiniums too.
The last of the seeds came today - all but Cooks - havent ordered yet.

19

Our sunny kitchen windowsill is still glorified by large vases of evergreens and forced flowers which look all the fresher for the continuing frost outside.

19 94 Make a plan of what & when for April Plant Sale.

Finally got some rain (2/12 & 13) 1/4 inch - not much but better than nothing. Highs in the high 40's or low 50's; lows 38°-42°.

19 95 Need a grow light fixture - must buy before tomatos are 1" tall. Purchased & assembled last week of Feb - as of 3/4 still on dining room table - uncooperative mate.

19____

...st roses from J&P soon. Hope
...h growth habit data to allow
...t. - Arrived 2/9 - All Hybrid Teas
...aij 2/11
...ve order from Old Heirloom Garden
...k. Nope they will not ship til April
... Flower & Garden Show on 2/10. They
...not good. Tickets no longer for a
... no limit on number of people
...lt - much more crowded than
...n't even see the displays & the
...& forth ect) was very long & totally
...t oriental lilies from the Lily Pad
...k. Need to plant today 2/11.

...NCULA
...ERIES

04-16-94 4
14-23 0031

3 •1•69I
4 X
•1•19 a
2 •4•76I
2 X
•0•79 a
2 •1•58I
•8•03I TA
•0•62I TX

•8•65M

In the garden, it is interesting to observe that many of the herbs, true culinary ones, which were crammed anyhow into hastily made borders last year, stand out most pleasantly even in the deeps of winter. Silver-stemmed lavender, spreading puddles of curly leafed golden marjoram, and spiky, distinctive mounds of rosemary all stand up to maritime winters with aplomb.

LATE FEBRUARY

A site that is open to light in winter and spring but shaded by deciduous shrubs or trees in summer allows small bulbs to be mixed in plentifully. The textures of unfolding fern foliage suit the delicacy of crocus, tiny tulips, and miniature daffodils better than coarser large-leafed companions do. If your shady place gets too little direct light for small bulbs, pink or coppery primroses will help draw the eye to the emerging fronds. Such details add immeasurably to the overall quality of a garden.

19*94* Must have been busy this last period since I didnt take time to write. Lots of Seeds are planted - most are up.

19*95*

19____

NOTES

Tiny reticulated iris are electrifying in late winter, delicate yet bold. The flowers rise naked and gleaming in the thin winter sunshine, colored egg-yolk yellow, lustrous purple, gentle or lucid blue. If you pot up the bulbets in rich soil and keep them outside, sheltering in a cold frame or trench (or in the sandbox), you can bring these fragrant gems indoors when they bloom, the better to appreciate the delicacy of their fine markings.

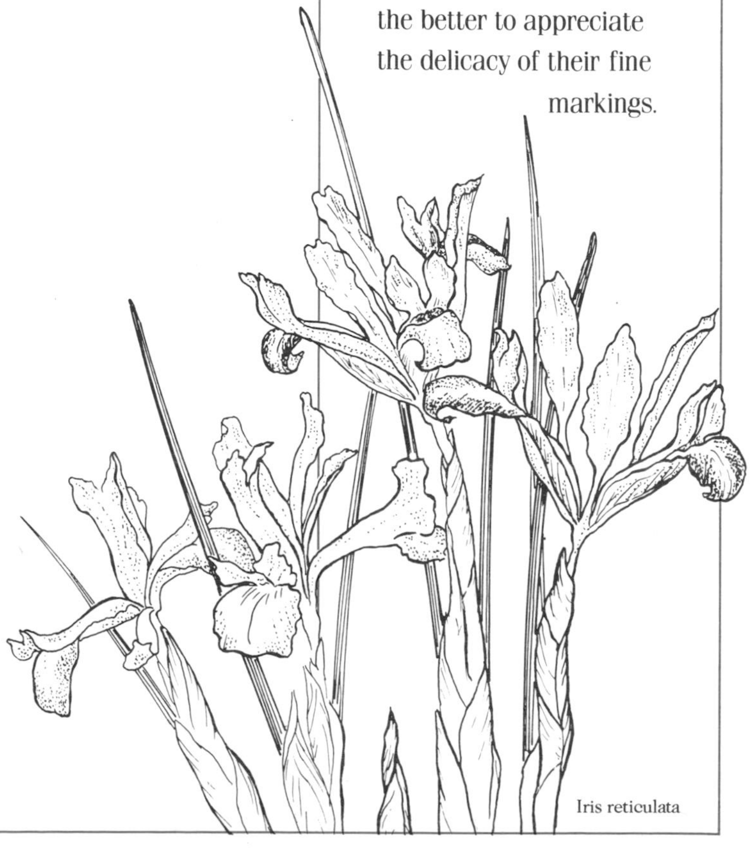

Iris reticulata

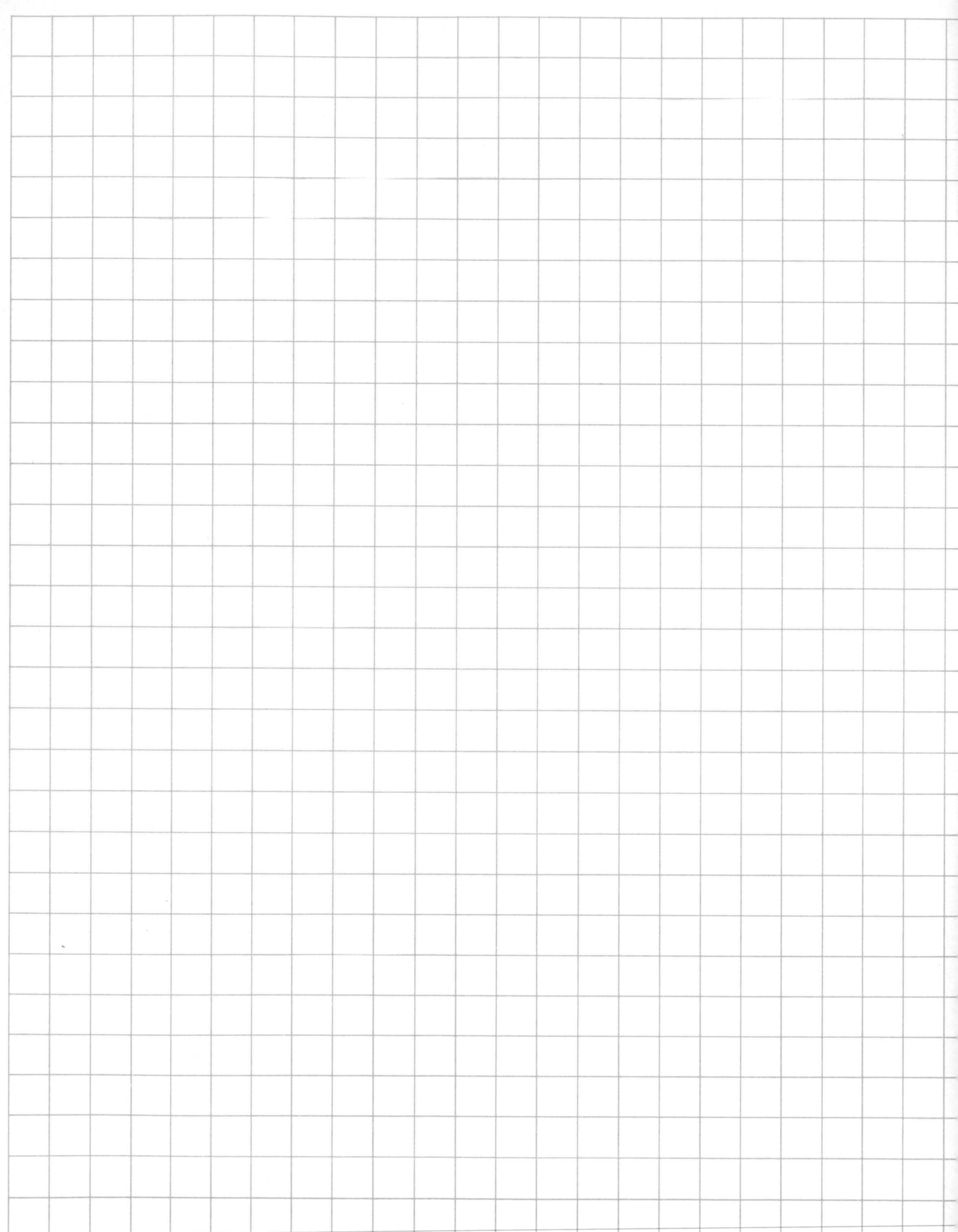

PLAN

NOTES

The inevitable wind and rain of coastal springs can wreak havoc with the taller daffodils and tulips. Spreading a mulch will reduce mud splashing, and planting shorter, more windproof varieties is equally good strategy. To avoid starting a slug farm, use rough shredded bark rather than leaves for your mulch. When the first shoots are well up, scatter the bark with a lavish hand. This is a pleasant task; each tender leaf is an intimation of delights to come, and protecting future flowers makes us feel virtuous and clever at the same time.

19_____

19_____

19_____

Single early tulip 'Christmas Gold'

MARCH RECORD

19 94

		Date Completed
Projects and Chores	Start tomato, basil,	2/28
	Iris due from White Flower Farms	Here 3/16
	Potatoes due from Ronningers 3/15	Here 3/3
		Planted 3/7?

(Planting, pruning, weeding, watering, fertilizing, pest control)

Weather

(Temperature high and low, precipitation, unusual conditions)

19 95

		Date Completed
Projects and Chores	Start tomatoes,	3/8?
	Fertilize lawn & rhodys	Lawn 3/12
	Install grow light	3/11/95

(Planting, pruning, weeding, watering, fertilizing, pest control)

Weather Starting off clear & cold at nite - sprinkled 3/4 am.
Windy, windy, windy - some calm sunny days in 55+°

(Temperature high and low, precipitation, unusual conditions)

19____

Date Completed

Projects and Chores

(Planting, pruning, weeding, watering, fertilizing, pest control)

Weather

(Temperature high and low, precipitation, unusual conditions)

1994 Need to prepare potato beds. Till and add peat moss & fertilizer. Soil test reflects a need for P&K. Nitrogen is fine. Since the balance is right for the soils need & will add more acid, I'm going to use the 'old' rhody fertilizer on a couple of varieties (&)
Best laid plans & all . . . the potatoes are here 2 weeks early.

1995 Everything seems early first tulip out 3/18. Peas up 3/16 both sweet & garden. Got lots started in greenhouse. Tomatoes, onions butterfly weed (white), zinnias, foxglove, flax (blue & white), broccoli, lettuce, delphinium (yellow) heliotrope, annual euphorbia, impatiens
The tomatoes have true leaves & need transplanting soon. First Rhody in bloom 3/20.
Marge Sullivan brought two starts of big pink single peony - looks like it has buds set! Potted up one for Mary (Stein).
The weeds are growing like crazy - dont know how I'll ever catch up.

19____

A month ago each flower stood out, a treasure of color in a grey and quiet landscape. Now things are leaping out of the ground, the air snaps with electricity, and the garden is a vital, rapidly changing place. As the perennials wake up, their crowns are expanding daily.

One of the best recent tulip introductions is the absolutely delectable 'Sweetheart'. Egg-shaped green buds soften to shimmering yellow, edges feathered with angelic white wings. The slanted light of spring makes them translucent, almost supernal. Despite this ethereal appearance, they have a blessedly robust constitution, lasting well both cut and in the border, and coming back strongly each year.

19 94 The weather has been very nice but no rain (1/10 in so far). Turned on Soaker hose (300') Sat 3/12 & Sunday. Got some of the lawn edged 3/13. Transplanted unhappy campers on 3/12 - Pittosporum to hill, Rhody 'Yak' to hill. Carpenteria to bed south of bedroom. Also planted the bush morning glories - Something in the greenhouse has got to go - need space for seedlings - the osteospermum will go next. Started hardening them off 3/12. Potted raspberries for plant sale 3/12. Moved compost pile from bin one to two 3/12.

No wonder I'm tired!

19 95
Picked up an order at Arrowswood Nursery on 3/2. Most still sitting on greenhouse steps. Need serious soil improvement on west side of drive about half way down. At the moment (3/9) there is a load of compost in the wheel barrow. Its too cold to do anything - rain, grey & wind.

19____

Potatoes due 3/15. Here 3/3 Planted 3/7
Greenhouse seedlings include 73 tomato plants OG50, Oregon Spring, Early Girl, Chico III (paste), & Fantastic. Also some T&M specials called Sungold just now coming up.
Sifted compost & planted roses 3/16 (Parks). Iris arrived from White Flower Farms today also. Need to get them in tomorrow.

To really get the timing right, it helps to keep garden notes as the flowers open. Which blossoms coincide? Which overlap? What blooms first, and when does it usually start? Which colors complement, which clash or fail to please? It doesn't need to be a major undertaking; even quite sketchy information and dates can still be useful.

LATE MARCH

Clematis montana is now in full bloom, a great glory of pale blossoms. It has built up to this performance over the past month and will continue well into May, with a light spangling of flowers all summer and a lesser, farewell display in the fall. Just now one can hardly see the leaves for the closely packed flowers. These look a bit like dogwood with their four rounded petals. They open white, but with age turn ivory-pink and become flushed with lavender along the slightly ruffled edges. Like anemones, they have a thick, fluffy-central puff of stamens, here in palest yellow, and the whole blossom is faintly tinged with green. This is a flower to savor and appreciate at close hand, a few floating in a flat bowl or tucked with a sprig of leaves into a desk-top bud vase for inspiration.

1994 The weather is finally looking up. Early in the week it snowed, hailed, sleeted, rained & the sun shown. Then we had two cold nights 30° or lower. Now on Thurs. it was 50+ and will be getting warmer thru the first part of next week.

The peonies I got from Shirley are doing great. They are sending up loads of fat buds.

1995 This last week Feb seems to be the point at which I give in to the "lets get started" urge. Peas & sweet peas are in, Spinach & Sweetness II carrot also. In the green house several annuals & perennials have been seeded & come up. The last day 28th I also started a couple of six packs of lettuce to transplant under the pea tent. As of 3/3 the lettuce is up already.

19____

David Tarrant UBC Vancouver, Ca
Home Remedies Sat 3/4/95.

1) Sprinkle freshly used coffee grounds down rows of carrots every 10 days to deter carrot fly.

2) Mildew & black spot 1 tsp baking soda a couple of shavings of bar soap & a half gallon or so of water - mix & spray on affected plants.

3) Crushed egg shells around seedling for cut worms.

4) veg oil 1 TBSP
molasses 1 TBS
yeast 1 tsp
water 1 cup
mix, place 1/4 in in old tin cans burried in garden to rim for earwigs

5) Mealy bugs
1 litre water
3/4 drops corn oil / vegi oil 1 ~~TBSP~~ tsp
3 drops dishwashing liquid
mix & spray

6) White fly
dust buster & sticky traps

Clematis montana

PLAN

PHOTOGRAPHS

NOTES

Once you get started with composting, you will wonder how you ever gardened without it. There is no better soil builder, and many plants like tree peonies and bulbs which resent animal manures benefit visibly from this "plant manure." Intensively planted flower beds perform far better with generous additions of compost; the plants grow and bloom well, yet require far less fertilizer than usual. Ongoing applications of compost result in an open, humusy soil that promotes extensive root development. In such conditions, plants establish and reach blooming size faster.

19____

19____

19____

Cytisus scoparius 'Moonlight'

APRIL RECORD

19____

Date Completed

Projects and Chores

Plant tomatoes — 4/19
1 Siberian 2 OG50
1 Early Swedish 1 Early Girl 1 Sungold
1 ? Early Girl ? 1 Chico III (1 Pink Brandywine 5/02)

(Planting, pruning, weeding, watering, fertilizing, pest control)

Weather

I know we had some but . . . must have been fairly normal.

(Temperature high and low, precipitation, unusual conditions)

19____

Date Completed

Projects and Chores

Plant Sale April 22nd
Cut off old perennial stocks — 4/3
Cut back butterfly bushes — 4/1

(Planting, pruning, weeding, watering, fertilizing, pest control)

Weather

Temperature this month was above normal & then below normal. Had maybe one frost and almost no measurable rain - hoses & sprinklers already out & in use.

(Temperature high and low, precipitation, unusual conditions)

19____

Date Completed

Projects and Chores

(Planting, pruning, weeding, watering, fertilizing, pest control)

Weather

(Temperature high and low, precipitation, unusual conditions)

19 94

This journal reflects how busy I was. I never had the time or remembered it. 8 days were spent in Arizona - three at mom's, several at the garden club & the rest here pulling weeds, planting etc.

19 ____

19 ____

Most of us have some sentimental favorites among the old-fashioned plants. Hollyhocks may remind us of making dolls in Grandmother's garden. The roses and violets, lavenders and mints that grew in the neighborhood are the very stuff of childhood, forever linked with our discovery of scents, textures, flavors.

19<u>94</u> Heirloom Old Garden Roses due 4/15

19____

19____

MID-APRIL

The most delightful spring-flowering shrub of all has got to be the 'Moonlight' broom. It is at its peak from April into May, a perfect explosion of popcorn flowers in butter yellow—but that doesn't do it justice. Prom-gown yellow, lemon-ice yellow, moonlight yellow. . . it's definitely not pastel, but if ever a color was both pale and bright, this is it. The shrub seems full of light, the flowers bubbling off the arching sprays in such abundance that the branches are invisible.

LATE APRIL

The season in which you prune lilac is relatively unimportant, so have a stab at it whenever you feel the urge (or get up your nerve). Deadheading, cutting off the faded flower trusses, does not affect floral display in subsequent years, whatever you may read to the contrary. If the faded flowers offend you, however, you may pluck them out. Left on the shrub, the seedheads attract many birds in winter, a bright ornament to any garden. If you feel lazy, you may explain to those who chivvy you about the untrimmed lilac that you are motivated by ecological concerns to leave those seedheads in place.

19~~95~~ 4/20
Busy, busy - finally ready for the plant sale. It will take 3 vehicles full to get it all up to the clubhouse. The Villager & the T. P U
Since most effort was expended for the sale, the weeds are getting the best of me. But today the rhodys are starting to open. Williamsianum & its cousin are finished already. The two new bunches of tulips I planted last fall (Monte Carlo & Angelique) are beautiful! Both are multi blossomed and are lasting well in spite of the awful wind of last nite.

19____

19____

NOTES

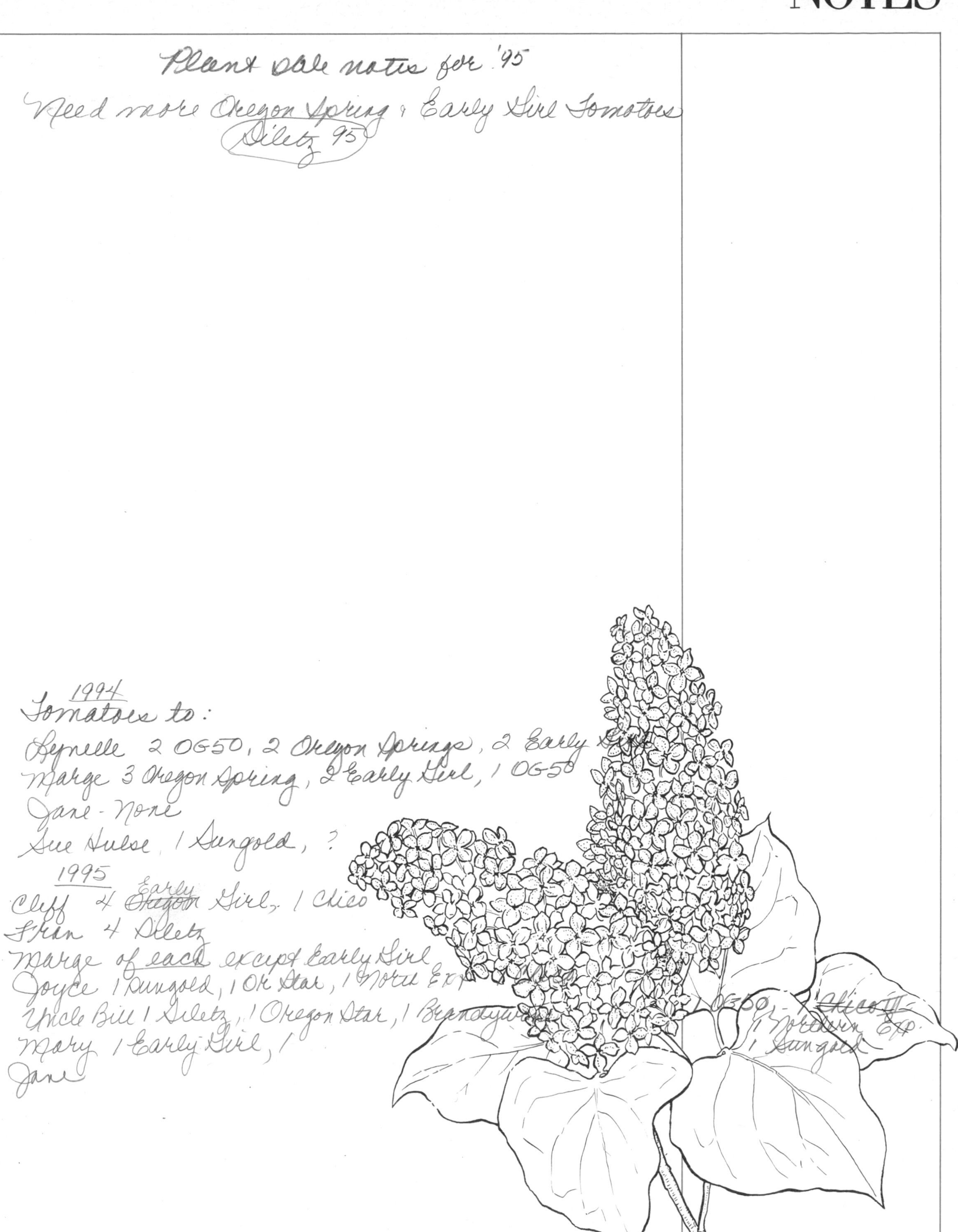

Plant sale notes for '95

Need more Oregon Spring & Early Girl Tomatoes

(Siletz 95)

1994

Tomatoes to:

Lynelle 2 OG50, 2 Oregon Springs, 2 Early Girl

Marge 3 Oregon Spring, 2 Early Girl, 1 OG50

Jane - None

Sue Hulse, 1 Sungold, ?

1995

Cliff 4 ~~Oregon~~ Early Girl, 1 Chico

Fran 4 Siletz

Marge of each except Early Girl

Joyce 1 Sungold, 1 Or Star, 1 North Exp

Uncle Bill 1 Siletz, 1 Oregon Star, 1 Brandywine, 1 OG50, 1 ~~Chico III~~ 1 Northern Exp. 1 Sungold

Mary 1 Early Girl, 1

Jane

Syringa vulgaris, lilac

PLAN

NOTES

As you weed, every inch of each bed gets scrutinized, an easy task when each emerging crown, each plump bud, each swelling shoot stands out clearly against bare soil or mulch. There is great delight in renewing our acquaintance with the burgeoning garden, and there's no better time to get the jump on those wheeling weeds.

19____

19____

19____

Basil, cherry tomato, fennel, butter lettuce, chives, and oregano

MAY RECORD

19 94

Date Completed

Projects and Chores

	Date Completed
Plant beans & pumpkins	5/10
Plant sunflowers	5/10
Plant all the stuff around in pots	5/29
Used Lilly Miller Vegie Dust for cutworms, etc.*	5/29
Put diatomatious earth on strawberries	5/29
Spray for deer	5/2 & 5/30

(Planting, pruning, weeding, watering, fertilizing, pest control)

Weather

Beautiful weather over Mother's Day weekend 68°-72°
Week of 5/20 thru 5/28 wind blew awfully hard. Cold
some rain 1/10"
Earlier this month we had 1/2 inch of rain

(Temperature high and low, precipitation, unusual conditions)

* on pumpkins, artichokes, sunflowers, peppers, tomatoes & bean

19 95

Date Completed

Projects and Chores

Plant Beans & pumpkins
Plant Sunflowers
Plant Squash

(Planting, pruning, weeding, watering, fertilizing, pest control)

Weather

(Temperature high and low, precipitation, unusual conditions)

19____

Date Completed

Projects and Chores

(Planting, pruning, weeding, watering, fertilizing, pest control)

Weather

(Temperature high and low, precipitation, unusual conditions)

EARLY MAY

19*94*____

19____

19____

May is a month of blobby bloomers, shapeless but willing. There is, however, great beauty in the flowing rivers and spreading carpets, low mounds and creeping mats of midspring color. The scene as a whole is soft-edged, gentle, promising with fast-developing shoots. This makes for quiet charm rather than high and vivid contrast; lovers of the overblown must wait till June for opulence.

19~~94~~

Found the killdeer nest in the yard 5/15. Put some sticks around it since they made it in the middle of the bark near the Braeburn apple tree. Its a wonder I didnt step in it or drop tools on it while planting the Great Northern potatoes several days earlier. Speaking of potatoes the ones planted at the base of the hill are doing great. One plant is getting ready to bloom (5/26).

19____

19____

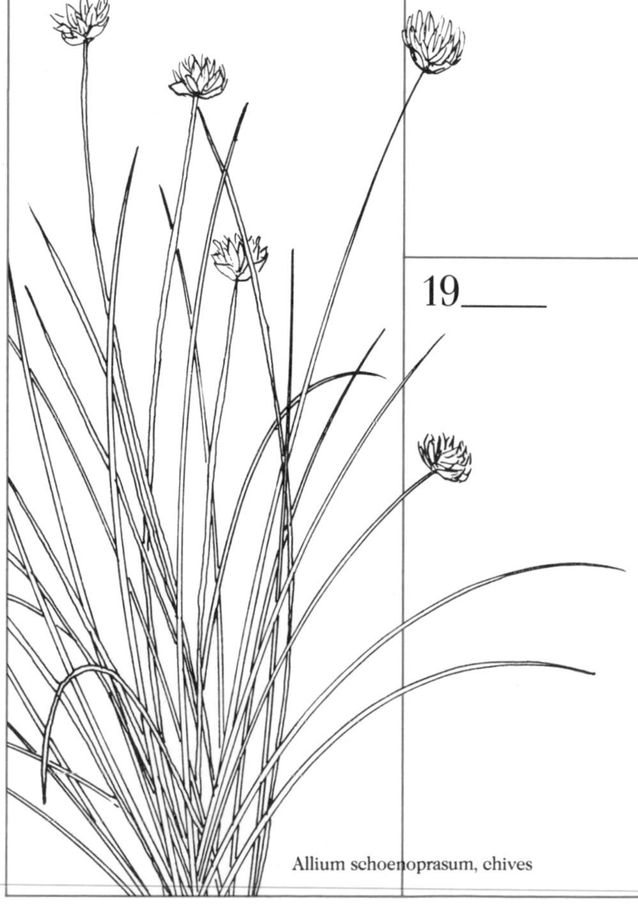

Allium schoenoprasum, chives

1994

All pine trees are sending out healthy long candles, even the shore pine that leaned first east, then west, as a result of the wind. It seems to have fixed its problem this spring. Recent winds haven't bothered it. The grand/silver? fir I moved this spring (early) is putting out good growth also. The coast redwoods look awful again this spring. If they dont recover nicely they will be history – The giant redwood is very happy & healthy & now has a mate.

Peach tree has curl again & didnt bloom this year either (year #3).

A salad tub is perfect for a sunny spot. Lime green butter lettuce with ruffled pink radicchio, ferny fronds of dill and fennel, delicate sprays of salad burnet mingle pleasantly. Aromatic garlic chives, their huge white flower heads humming with bees, trailing oregano with rosy blooms, wide mounds of tiny-leaved basil, or bushy sheaves of the taller kinds all do well in such a position. Further color and scent come from lemon thyme, grey tarragon, and vigorous 'Whirlybird' nasturtiums. Train some 'Sweet 100' cherry tomatoes up a little trellis with 'Patio Pik' cucumbers and a few 'Scarlet Runner' or tender haricot beans.

LATE MAY

One of the charms of peonies is their tantalizing swiftness: the buds burgeon, burst, bloom, and fade as quickly as fleeting spring itself leads us on to high summer. Gardeners who want more can choose early and late varieties, as well as the more common June bloomers, and can plant their peonies in partial shade to prolong the flowers as well.

19 94

All in all the flowers look fairly good. The wind did knock over a few things & the rain .5" a week or so ago knocked down the oriental poppies & some Shirleys. Think about peony cages for the orientals next year.
Deer came 5/2? and ate most of the pie cherry tree, some of the Black Republican & a good part of 4 roses (Roseraie, Unforgettable, Prince Camille De Rohan & Barbara Bush. Somehow they missed the J&P test roses, thank God! I sprayed that day with Hinder & put the wind chimes back together & on the pie cherry tree.

19____

19____

NOTES

Paeonia 'Sea Shell'

PLAN

NOTES

Arch and trellis are smothered with rapidly expanding leaves, swelling buds, and tentative, half-opened flowers. The paths and borders are filling to the bursting point; don't sigh for April or pant longingly for June, simply look at May and be glad.

19 94

The sweet peas planted on the west fence are not doing well. The soil probably needs improvement. The sweet peas planted on the South (brick) wall of the greenhouse are doing much better. However the moon flowers & morning glory vines I planted at least 3 weeks ago are not up - Need to replant both.

Took yard pictures 5/29

19____

19____

Tall bearded iris 'Ovation'

JUNE RECORD

19____

Date Completed

Projects and Chores

Write in this book!
Harvest 1st tomato (Early Swedish)

(Planting, pruning, weeding, watering, fertilizing, pest control)

Weather

(Temperature high and low, precipitation, unusual conditions)

19____

Date Completed

Projects and Chores

(Planting, pruning, weeding, watering, fertilizing, pest control)

Weather

(Temperature high and low, precipitation, unusual conditions)

19____

Date Completed

Projects and Chores

(Planting, pruning, weeding, watering, fertilizing, pest control)

Weather

(Temperature high and low, precipitation, unusual conditions)

EARLY JUNE

19____

19____

19____

An astonishing number of plants will thrive on the mixture of sun and shade offered by most yards. Only experimentation and time will tell you the perfect combinations for your particular site. Fortunately, the process is enormously stimulating, the disasters relatively cheap and quickly hustled away. Visits to other gardens lead to fresh ideas, trips to local nurseries leave you with a new treasure trove, a wave of the gardener's trowel makes all good, and if it doesn't, well, you have the joys of endless new beginnings ahead.

19____
19____
19____

MID-JUNE

Is there anything more spectacular than the bearded iris in their short season? The newer varieties command our attention, as compellingly attractive as royalty. In fact, they have much the same air of gracious majesty as the Queen Mother, and much the same taste in hats. Perhaps it's that they look rather like her hats, especially those enormous, ruffled ones worn at the famous summer teas.

LATE JUNE

There is something rather touching about the first tiny zucchini. It is so small, so tender, so innocent-looking. It is the harbinger of full summer, the herald of wonderful things to come, and like many a cutie it can develop into an oversized monster overnight. The obvious course is to eat it before it multiplies.

19____

19____

19____

NOTES

'Cocozelle' zucchini

PLAN

PHOTOGRAPHS

NOTES

When you finally get started on that vacation, keep your eyes open for garden tours, and make a point of visiting nurseries wherever you go. It can be fascinating to see how foreign familiar plants can appear in another climate or setting. There is always the chance of seeing plants read about but never seen, or discovering flowers you've never even heard about. Each locale seems to favor certain plants and treatments, and it is refreshing to see new choices.

19____

19____

19____

Hemerocallis 'Ice Carnival'

JULY RECORD

19____

Date Completed

Projects and Chores

(Planting, pruning, weeding, watering, fertilizing, pest control)

Weather

(Temperature high and low, precipitation, unusual conditions)

19____

Date Completed

Projects and Chores

(Planting, pruning, weeding, watering, fertilizing, pest control)

Weather

(Temperature high and low, precipitation, unusual conditions)

19____

Date Completed

Projects and Chores

(Planting, pruning, weeding, watering, fertilizing, pest control)

Weather

(Temperature high and low, precipitation, unusual conditions)

19____

19____

19____

As summer matures, the border achieves ripe fullness and all the work of fall and spring shows results, good or bad. It's time to take a few pictures and to analyze—just a little—the overall effect. Make note of favorite combinations, and try to figure out just what makes them so good: color, texture, shape, contrast, or just plain delightful plants. If there are large blanks in the border, gaps or dull spots, note that too, so you can arrange some excitement for next year.

It's time to loosen up the old throwing arm and get out the binoculars. Summer is back, the flowers are flourishing, and the war is on. Urban gardeners may not have to worry much about deer or rabbits, but there are other forms of fauna quite as bad from which city gardens need zealous guarding. Cats, dogs, squirrels, and other terrorists abound, each worse than the other. Would-be guerrilla gardeners need a wide-ranging arsenal to be ready to face the foe of the hour. A stock of whiffle balls, perhaps kept in an attractive basket on the back porch. A whistle, the louder the better. Bird glasses, if you are part of a neighborhood Garden Watch network. Various repellent sprays.

19____

19____

19____

MID-JULY

Among modern daylilies an excellent performer is 'Ice Carnival', a crisp lemon-juice white with a small, brilliant, enamel green heart. The petals are as stiff as heavy silk, ruffled and fluted and diamond dusted to boot. 'Ice Carnival' blooms for most of the summer and opens late to perfume the evening air with its deep, sweet scent.

LATE JULY

Another good performer for the sunny border is Russian sage, *Perovskia atriplicifolia*, a silver blue bush with aromatic, downy leaves used to flavor vodka. Like caryopteris, Russian sage is delicate and light in appearance, a gentle haze of lavender blue billowing out perhaps three feet in all directions. The violet flowers are small, grouped on whorled spikes which contrast vividly in both form and color with the finely dissected smoky leaves.

1994
Mom & I took a trip to St Paul, Or to visit Heirloom Old Garden Roses. Oh so lovely - make you want one of everything. Weather was very warm. Conventions in the Portland area left nary a motel room to be had. Thank heavens someone with a reservation in Williams didnt show & we got their room. Had a great time. Stopped at Paul & Jaynes on the way home.

19____

19____

NOTES

Perovskia atriplicifolia, Russian sage

PLAN

NOTES

Full summer brings respite to the busy gardener. All the chores and activities of spring are finished (or left, too late, for fall. . .or next year). Trees and shrubs have leaved out, baskets are full of bloom, wave succeeds wave of color and scent in the full, fat borders. Time to sit back, relax, and enjoy the progression of bloom.

19____

19____

19____

Artemisia 'Silver Bouquet'

AUGUST RECORD

19____

Date Completed

Projects and Chores

The FAIR — 8/

(Planting, pruning, weeding, watering, fertilizing, pest control)

Weather

(Temperature high and low, precipitation, unusual conditions)

19____

Date Completed

Projects and Chores

(Planting, pruning, weeding, watering, fertilizing, pest control)

Weather

(Temperature high and low, precipitation, unusual conditions)

19____

Date Completed

Projects and Chores

(Planting, pruning, weeding, watering, fertilizing, pest control)

Weather

(Temperature high and low, precipitation, unusual conditions)

EARLY AUGUST

19____

19____

19____

Interesting bone structure gives definition, character, and sometimes beauty to a face from youth into old age, and so it is with gardens. Garden "bones" are delineators: paths, edgings, hedges, and certain plants, whether massive, solid, or tall. Such things direct the eye and guide, entice, or beckon the visitor on. Even the tiniest garden has need of such structure and will benefit appreciably from the judicious use of non-plant material as well as those special plants which give panache without overwhelming the smaller scene.

The neutrals of the garden color scheme play the same role in the border that they do in our wardrobes. Plants with foliage of grey, silver, and white add sparkle and important contrast to strong color combinations. When the molten meets the smoldering, the result can be disappointingly subfusc. Bold colors often cancel each other out; instead of building heat upon heat to explosive visual fireworks, the picture fizzles, a sullen dud. It takes the greys of ash and smoke to set off the jets of hot color; diluted with silver and grey, bright colors are intensified and the scene achieves full strength.

19____

19____

19____

MID-AUGUST

Making a garden is a lengthy process—it takes a lifetime of experimentation. Gradually you adjust your collection to include things you admire, editing out the dull or unsuccessful, allowing time for plants to mature, to display their full potential. The net result is an intensely personal statement, a living, changing, breathing garden.

LATE AUGUST

Common as daisies, cosmos fill the same garden niche from late summer until fall's last gasp. Sun-colored mixtures were born to blend with rusty, tawny fall-toned chrysanthemums. The pure-white strain adds depth and sparkle to a bed of blazing dahlias. The curled, tubular petals of the cosmos 'Sea Shells' come in a pastel-pretty range; for a lovely, long-lasting display, back a generous sweep with the tall artemisia 'Lad's Love' and set a band of low border dahlias in lavender, cream, and rose at its feet.

19<u>94</u> Vegi Summary.

In spite of the crazy summer weather - cold, hot, cold hot, wind, wind, wind, most of the tomatoes did fairly well. The best were Sungold cherry & OG50. Red Brandywine should have been started earlier as not many ripened. Carrots were good early & then the carrot fly hit. Peppers did suprisingly well. They were in water walls till late July. Each plant set a couple of peppers that ripened. Potatoes didnt produce well with the exception of Great Northern. Peas were eaten by Foxy in Apr. Zucchini produced well but winter squash was worse than so-so. Asparagus were wonderful! Put a heap of seaweed on in Sept.

19____

19____

Cosmos 'Bright Lights'

PLAN

NOTES

There are some fetching culinary uses for summer flowers; pinky pale shrimp tumbling from purple daylily cornucopias or Latin-bright nasturtiums floating in gazpacho can zip up a basic menu. Stuffed nasturtiums make nice tidbits, too; run some ricotta and smoked salmon through the blender, chop in toasted hazelnuts and a sprig of fennel, add a squeeze of lemon juice —perfect!

19 94 Vegi Summary (contd)

Strawberries should be replaced – Burpee has a variety "Shortcake" thats red all the way thru.

Raspberry cross pole fell down in Aug. Need to have a new one.

Only Red Grav. apple produced fruit. About 8 apples to be eaten.

19____

19____

Sorbus aucuparia, mountain ash

SEPTEMBER RECORD

19____

Date Completed

Projects and Chores

(Planting, pruning, weeding, watering, fertilizing, pest control)

Weather

(Temperature high and low, precipitation, unusual conditions)

19____

Date Completed

Projects and Chores

(Planting, pruning, weeding, watering, fertilizing, pest control)

Weather

(Temperature high and low, precipitation, unusual conditions)

19____

Date Completed

Projects and Chores

(Planting, pruning, weeding, watering, fertilizing, pest control)

Weather

(Temperature high and low, precipitation, unusual conditions)

19____

19____

19____

Restraint has its place, but surely not in the fall, when most of our gardens need all the oomph we can muster. No, no, forget restraint; let's go for the gold. And the silver. And the bronze. And the copper. . . .

The garden is alive with birds. Dozens, even hundreds, of them are busily foraging through the garden borders. The shrubs and small trees of the mixed border provide welcome cover for small birds. They all come to feast on the berries which linger in leafless swags on vines and trees throughout this crowded old garden. Gardeners who enjoy the company of birds during the winter and would like to encourage more of them to frequent the garden would do well to grow many such berrying plants. Come fall and winter, the unexpected flashes of color will brighten the fading scene.

19____

19____

19____

MID-SEPTEMBER

LATE SEPTEMBER

Garden-hopping gives you a great opportunity to see unfamiliar plants in a garden setting, important because a specimen in a pot at a nursery is still essentially an unknown. It isn't until you see an established plant in a garden, among companions, that you get a real sense of its potential, how it relates to other plants, its presence or personality, and where it might appear to greatest advantage in your own garden.

19____

19____

19____

NOTES

If you love the outrageous look of the big dahlias, but regretfully decline them because they don't fit into your overall garden scheme, put some in the cutting garden. The more splendiferous dahlias are terrific with fall foliage in arrangements, a distinct plus when garden pickings are few.

Dahlia 'Eveline'

PLAN

Sept 97

PHOTOGRAPHS

NOTES

The better we know our plants—their habits of growth, eventual sizes, propensities to sprawl or spread—the better we can place them where they can be "comfortable," letting them grow as they like without the need for constant pruning and restraint. Low, mounded edging plants should spill over the border edge onto the grass; grass is not holy, and the plant will look far prettier than when shorn back.

19____

19____

19____

Chrysanthemum 'Yellow Beam'

OCTOBER RECORD

19____

Date Completed

Projects and Chores

(Planting, pruning, weeding, watering, fertilizing, pest control)

Weather

(Temperature high and low, precipitation, unusual conditions)

19____

Date Completed

Projects and Chores

(Planting, pruning, weeding, watering, fertilizing, pest control)

Weather

(Temperature high and low, precipitation, unusual conditions)

19____

Date Completed

Projects and Chores

(Planting, pruning, weeding, watering, fertilizing, pest control)

Weather

(Temperature high and low, precipitation, unusual conditions)

EARLY OCTOBER

19____

19____

19____

October is the twilight of summer, a half-state in which deciduous trees slowly shed the year's leaves, their winter silhouettes emerging as the angle of the sunlight lengthens. For most of us, summer's end is the moment of truth; how do our gardens grow?

Spiky, punky spider chrysanthemums challenge the complacent look of the more common forms. 'Pink Pagoda' in flaming fuchsia makes a lovely counterpoint to the silky, broad petals of 'Alice', a silver pink double Japanese anemone. These plants both want all the room, and the two duke it out for space every year.

19____

19____

19____

MID-OCTOBER

As the air gets that crispy edge to it and fresh cider floods the market, the pungent, spicy scent of chrysanthemums pervades the garden. There are thousands of them now, from simple daisy shapcs to thc bizarrc Fujis, ornate, quilled spiders and spoons, huge football types with padded shoulders or the boudoir cushion, plump pillows solid with pompoms.

LATE OCTOBER

It is always a surprise to find the fat pink buds of the nerines shooting up in the late fall border. They appear, buxom and strapping, on thick stalks, very like the buds of their cousin, the amaryllis, that we grow indoors all winter. When the plump buds finally pop, the flowers emerge in hot pink starbursts, little curly lilies arranged in wide umbels, like those of agapanthus or flowering onion, but far jazzier.

19____

19____

19____

PLAN

NOTES

Making a new garden, or a new bed in an existing garden, is one of the most exciting processes there is. Doing this work in the fall is like making new wine; new soil also needs time to meld and mellow. Now the ground lies bare, bursting with possibilities, open to any interpretation you choose to impose upon it.

19____

19____

19____

Ampelopsis brevipedunculata 'Elegans'

NOVEMBER RECORD

19____

Date Completed

Projects and Chores

(Planting, pruning, weeding, watering, fertilizing, pest control)

Weather

Some cold weather mid month. Then fairly warm & rainy for Thanksgiving, Thank God!

(Temperature high and low, precipitation, unusual conditions)

19____

Date Completed

Projects and Chores

(Planting, pruning, weeding, watering, fertilizing, pest control)

Weather

(Temperature high and low, precipitation, unusual conditions)

19____

Date Completed

Projects and Chores

(Planting, pruning, weeding, watering, fertilizing, pest control)

Weather

(Temperature high and low, precipitation, unusual conditions)

EARLY NOVEMBER

19____

19____

19____

It is always a delight to stroll through the late-autumn garden, savoring each bit of color, marveling over every stalwart bloom. Even at this late date, and after a summer of stress, there is a remarkable amount of beauty in the yard. There are still some delightful combinations going.

The miniature Boston ivy, *Parthenocissus lowii*, has minute splay-fingered leaves barely an inch across. This one will embroider itself in a delicate tracery over a wall, ornamental as a tapestry. The new leaves are lacquered in fresh parsley green like little enameled badges. By autumn, they are richly tinted with a whole wide palate of gold, copper, bronze, and rust, with flaring flames of scarlet as fall deepens.

1994

19____

19____

MID-NOVEMBER

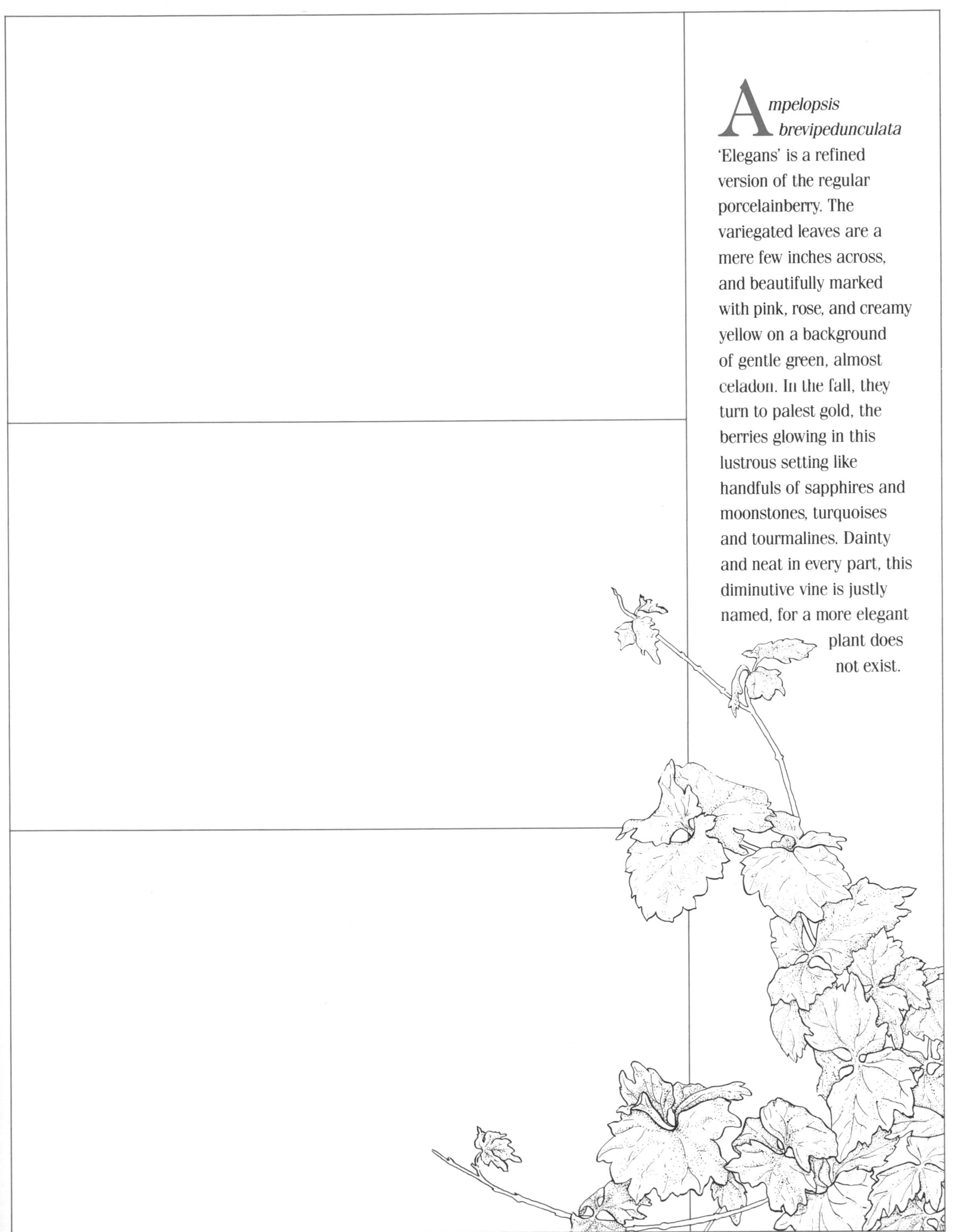

Ampelopsis brevipedunculata 'Elegans' is a refined version of the regular porcelainberry. The variegated leaves are a mere few inches across, and beautifully marked with pink, rose, and creamy yellow on a background of gentle green, almost celadon. In the fall, they turn to palest gold, the berries glowing in this lustrous setting like handfuls of sapphires and moonstones, turquoises and tourmalines. Dainty and neat in every part, this diminutive vine is justly named, for a more elegant plant does not exist.

LATE NOVEMBER

By November we're tired of chores and ready to appreciate arching sprays of toad lilies (*Tricyrtis* species), mottled purple or lilac or white, their curious curving stamens like a snail's horns. The persimmon-colored fruits of the stinking iris, *Iris foetidissima,* are cupped in their split tan sheaths, the carmine berries cluster thickly in little club-heads on the stout stems of Italian arums, *Arum italicum* 'Pictum'. The garden is full of subtle treasures and effects unknown to the incurably neat.

19____

19____

19____

NOTES

Tricyrtis hirta, toad lily

PLAN

NOTES

Even after weeks of light freezes, wind, and chilly rains, the garden still offers enough to make up delightful little posies, largely because the borders are not pruned to the ground in September. Most of the plants are left to fend for themselves and the protection of their own upper growth brings even quite tender things through very cold weather—if not unscathed, at least alive.

19____

19____

19____

DECEMBER

Galanthus nivalis, snowdrop

DECEMBER RECORD

19____

Date Completed

Projects and Chores

(Planting, pruning, weeding, watering, fertilizing, pest control)

Weather Lots of rain this month - Estimate 5 inches!
Warmer than normal after 1ST week.

(Temperature high and low, precipitation, unusual conditions)

19____

Date Completed

Projects and Chores

(Planting, pruning, weeding, watering, fertilizing, pest control)

Weather

(Temperature high and low, precipitation, unusual conditions)

19____

Date Completed

Projects and Chores

(Planting, pruning, weeding, watering, fertilizing, pest control)

Weather

(Temperature high and low, precipitation, unusual conditions)

1994 Cold weather - ice & snow 12/2, 3, 4.	Besides an extra degree of frost protection, the unkempt garden offers some positive pleasures. Dozens of birds enjoy the great variety of seeds, and their bickering and scraps of song sound cheerful on still, chilly mornings. Naked bushes shiver, ashimmer with silver floss where seedheads of intertwined clematis persist. Streams of thin winter sunshine reveal frost traceries along the veins of fallen leaves which lie in richly colored piles of mahogany, ebony, chestnut, and oak.
19____	
19____	

Snowdrops make frequent December appearances, each drooping bell closed tight against the cold. On sunny days they open wider, and you can see that each inner petal is marked with a tiny green fish. Portly yellow buds and Irish green stems of winter jasmine (*Jasminum nudiflorum*) lighten winter gloom in golden sunny sprays, a faint wild scent unfolding sporadically in a warm room.

19____

19____

19____

It is possible to own a lot full of trees without having much worth saving. In wooded areas, take advantage of the neighbors' trees, using them as "borrowed landscape" features, a technique seen in traditional Japanese gardens. You can largely clear your own property, using shrubs and smaller trees to frame views which include trees beyond the property lines as a focal point. Perfectly legal.

LATE DECEMBER

Each Christmas morning, our breakfast table is graced with a small bouquet. What began one balmy year as a celebration of the mildness of maritime Northwestern winters has become a tradition. The bouquet is rarely an impressive display, but the thrill of the hunt is a major part of the fun. The whole family enjoys searching the frosty borders for a few rimed buds, the whooping delight of a good find in an open year.	19____
	19____
	19____

Hardy cyclamen are miniature cousins of the exotic Persians we grow (or kill) in the house. Their scalloped, heart-shaped leaves are frequently marbled or stippled with soft patterning in cream or silver, making pleasant patterns when grown as a winter ground cover. The flowers open from whorled, tightly wrapped buds, as skinny as a stork's beak, and as they unwrap, they turn themselves inside out like little fluttering butterflies.

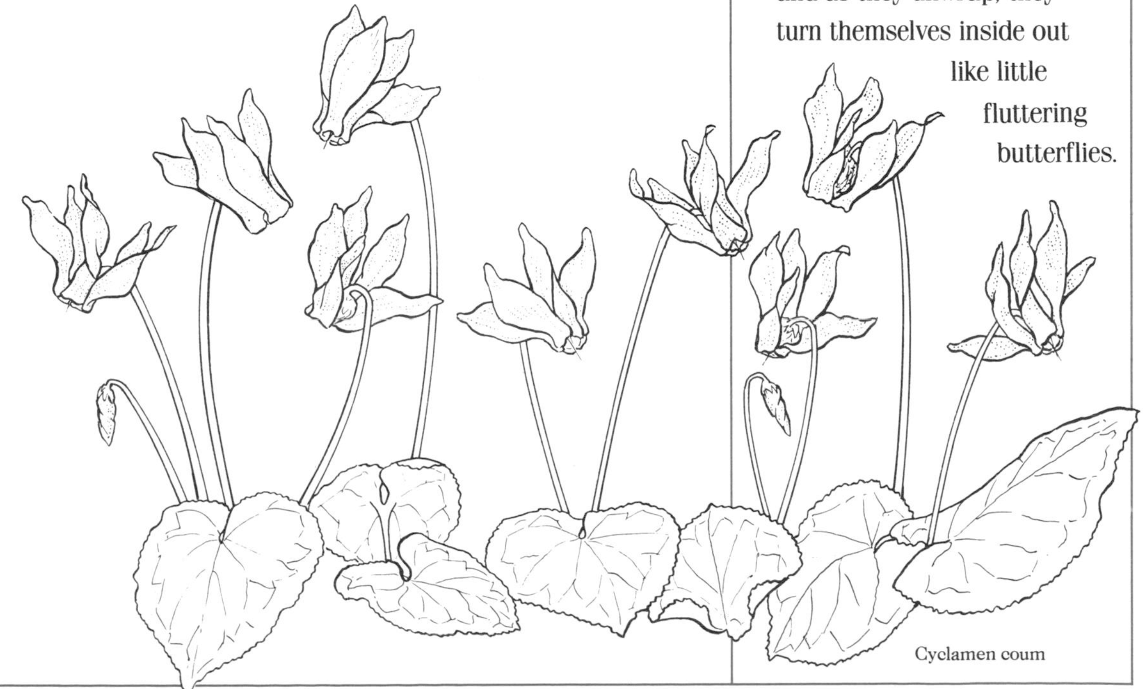

Cyclamen coum

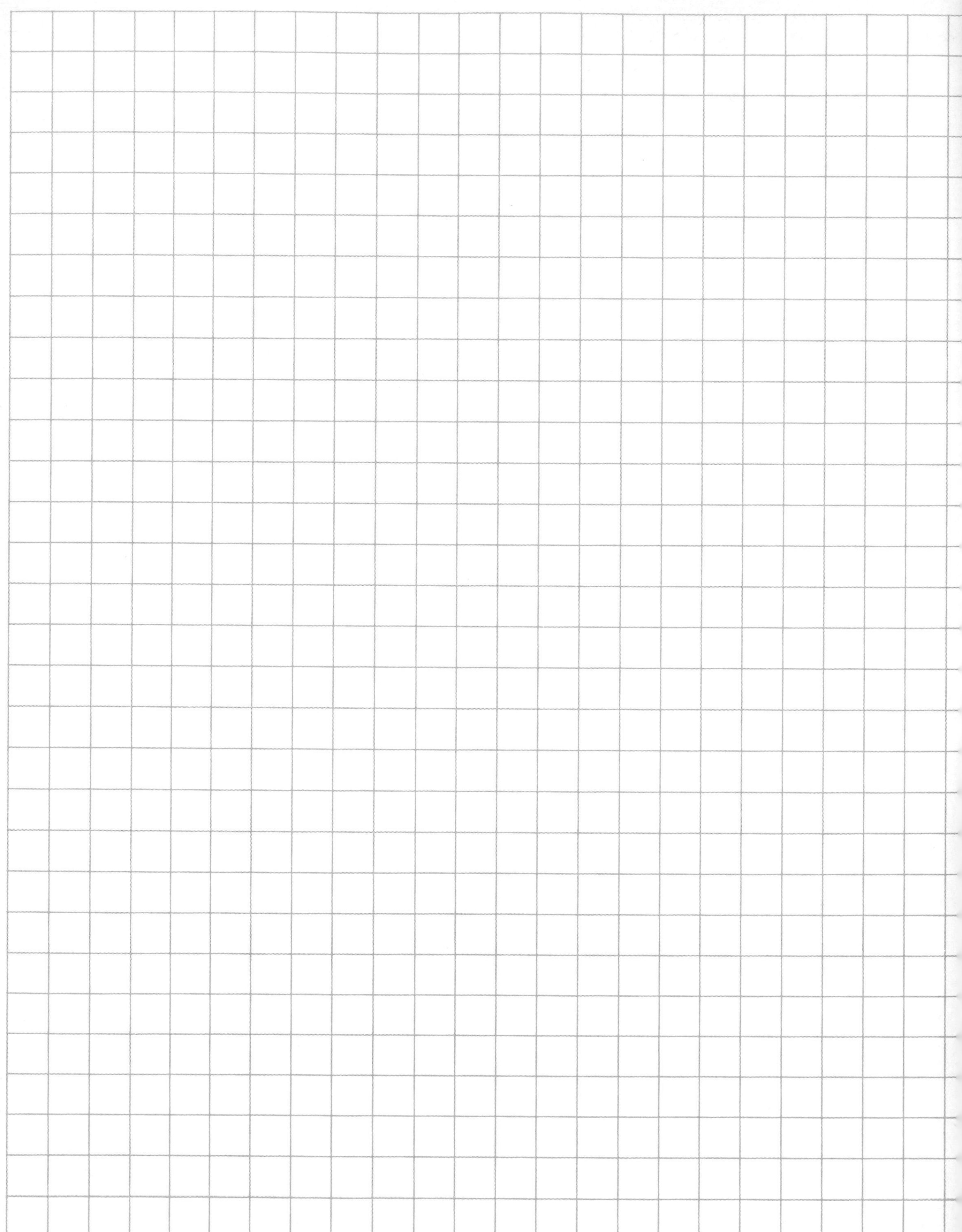

PLAN

Graham Thomas - Named in honor of the famed plantsman and rosarian

Mary Rose

Graham Thomas®

Named in honor of Graham Thomas, the great plantsman and rosarian who played a major part in restoring worldwide interest in the classic Old Roses, this splendid variety is acclaimed by some experts as the finest of all the David Austin roses. A sensation when first introduced at London's prestigious Chelsea Flower Show, it produces apricot buds that open to cupped- shaped flowers of rich, glistening yellow — a striking color rarely found in Old Roses. It performs marvelously despite heat and humidity, perfuming the air with its heady Tea fragrance. A vigorous yet elegant upright grower with light green foliage, growing 8 feet tall and 5 feet wide.

Mary Rose®

A true classic, with flowers of rich pink, with much of the beauty and charm, as well as the wonderful fragrance, of the old Damask roses. Neat and bushy, 4 feet by 4 feet, this robust shrub keeps on branching to produce new flowering shoots. One of the earliest of roses to begin flowering and one of the last to stop, it is rarely without bloom in between. May be pruned to any desired dimensions.

New English Rose Offer 42060-6

5 Plants — One each of Othello, Mary Rose, Heritage, Graham Thomas and Fair Bianca
Just check New English Rose offer box on your personal postpaid order card.

SEND NO MONEY NOW!

Just check your selections on the enclosed, postage-free order card and return it to us. We'll send your roses at the proper planting time for your area, along with an invoice for them. Examine the plants in the comfort of your home. If you're not entirely pleased, return them to us at our expense — you owe us nothing. And even after you've paid for your roses, planted and grown them, you're protected by:

Park's Risk-Free Guarantee

Every one of Park's Meidiland™ Family of Landscape Roses, Park's Old-Fashioned Roses and Park's New English Roses must grow and bloom to your satisfaction. If any should not, we'll replace it postpaid and free of charge, or refund its cost, whichever you prefer — just let us know by this coming October 1. Try them for yourself at no risk!

Order Today!

For all roses in this brochure, shipments start March 8th and stop the end of April. The time for ordering and shipping is short, so PLEASE ORDER NOW! Just fill out your enclosed personal order card and send it in TODAY!

Cokesbury Road, Greenwood, SC 29647-0001

David Austin's® New English Roses

This totally new class of Roses is the result of nearly 40 years of work by the renowned English rose breeder, David Austin. His goal was to create a new kind of rose — repeat flowering, disease-resistant shrubs, suitable for even the smaller gardens of today. To accomplish these ends, Austin used a rich mixture of parents — various old shrub roses for their vigor, fragrance, disease resistance, beauty of form and attractiveness of foliage; and Floribunda or Cluster Roses to add modern colors, scents, glossy foliage and, above all, the ability to flower continuously throughout the season. The results have been astounding and successful beyond Austin's wildest dreams — shrubs that are graceful, clad in lovely foliage, hardy and disease-resistant, and that abundantly bear flowers of exquisite form, color and fragrance throughout the season. These roses will add charm, beauty and distinction to your garden for years to come!

Othello

Heritage - Popular favorite of the Austin Collection

Fair Bianca

Heritage®

Everything a rose should be! Profusely borne in lovely sprays, the flowers have a perfection of form that is unequaled by any. The medium-sized, prettily cupped blossoms are of the clearest shell pink, and have a pronounced and unusual scent — that of Old Roses, with a strong overtone of lemon. They are generously produced throughout the summer in clusters. The plants are robust, compact and bushy, with strong, nearly thornless stems, and grow to 4 feet x 4 feet.

Othello®

(PP 7212) Very large, full-petaled flowers of cupped form that mature to extremely full, rounded blooms. One of the richest colored of the new English Roses, it is rich dark crimson which later turns to pleasing shades of purple and mauve. Habit is robust, upright and bushy, with numerous strong thorns and dusky, dark green foliage. Very resistant to pests and disease. Exceptionally free-flowering, with pronounced Old Rose fragrance. 5 feet x 5 feet.

Fair Bianca®

A pure white rose with flowers of the most exquisite Old Rose conformation, reminiscent of the Gallica Roses, centered with distinct green eyes. The round buds open to pretty little cups filled with petals, later becoming saucer-shaped and finally curving back at the edges and revealing green eyes in their centers. The blooms are perfumed with the fragrance of myrrh. This lovely rose is especially good for the small garden, as it grows to a compact 4 x 3 feet.

PHOTOGRAPHS

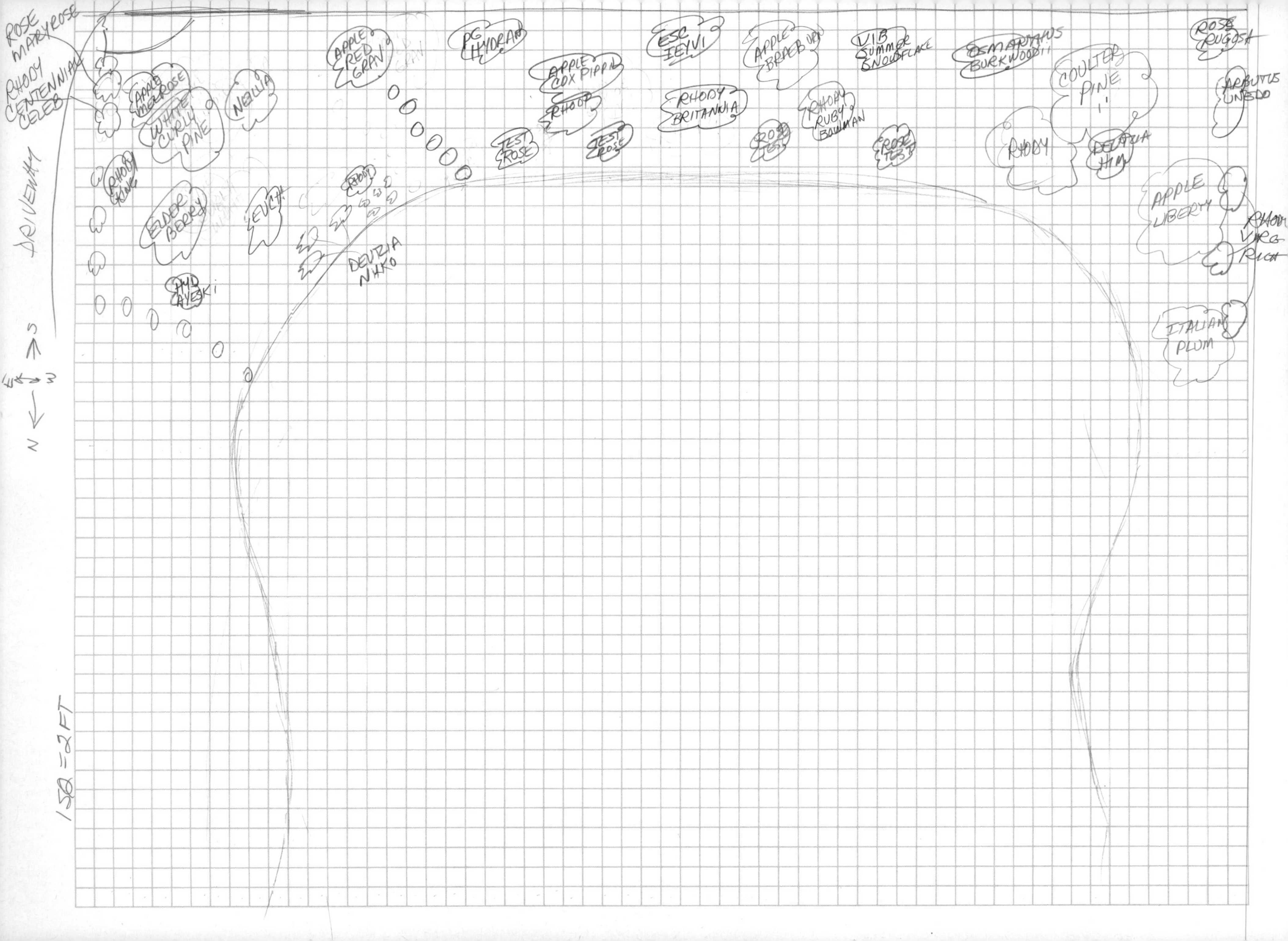

ROSE MARYROSE
RHODY CENTENNIAL CELEB
DRIVEWAY
N
S
E
W
APPLE MELROSE
WHITE CURLY PINE
NELLIA
RHODY KING
ELDER BERRY
EUCH
DEUTZIA NIKKO
APPLE RED GRAV
PG HYDRAN
TEST ROSE
APPLE COX PIPPIN
RHODY
ESC IEYVI
RHODY BRITANNIA
APPLE BRAEBURN
RHODY RUBY BOWMAN
VIB SUMMER SNOWFLAKE
OSMANTHUS BURKWOODII
COULTER PINE
RHODY
ROSE RUGOSA
ARBUTUS UNEDO
APPLE LIBERTY
ITALIAN PLUM
1SQ = 2FT

GARDEN PLAN

GARDEN PLAN

GARDEN PLAN

SUPPLIERS

Supplier Park Seed ($51.56)

Date ordered 12/27/93 **Date Received** 1/11/94

$	#	Name	Quality	Date planted OUT	Performance
5.99	7403	Canna Pfitzers Primrose Yellow		2/26	one seems rotten
✓ 9.95	6529-6	Miracle Mulch			
✓ 2.09	0997	Heuchera-Purple Palace	- Seed	5/94	Good
✓ 1.59	1113	Liatris-Spicta Kobold	- Seed	5/94	Slow !!!
✓ 1.95	1087	Knautia Macedonica	- Seed	4/94	Great. Still in bloom 1/2/95
✓ 1.55	0178	Arctotis Stoechadifolia	- Seed	4/94	Did well
✓ 1.99	0015	Aethionema Cordifolium	- Seed		
✓ 1.49	1352	Marigold Aurora Lt Yellow	- Seed	5/29/4	Good
✓ 1.39	5329	Tomato Early Girl	- Seed	4/18	Fair
✓ 1.59	5450	Tomato OG50	- Seed	4/18	Good
9.99	44856-5	Cortaderia Sunningdale Silver		2/280	Good
8.99	44061-0	Clematis montana rubens odorata	Died got refund	2/261	What a puny stick

Supplier Territorial Seed

Date ordered 12/28/93 ($12.65) **Date Received** 1/13/94

$	#	Name	Quality	Date planted	Performance
	ON550	Spanish Sweet Onion	- Seed	3/6	
	LT471	Little Gem Romaine	- Seed	3/6	OK
	PP620	Early Cal Wonder Pepper	- Seed	3/13*	GOOD
	PP621	Purple Beauty Pepper	- Seed	3/13*	GOOD
	KH432	Superschmelz Kohlrabi	- Seed		POOR
	BN126	Blue Lake Pole Beans	- Seed	5/10	GREAT
	FL3266	Sunflower - Sunseed	- Seed	5/10	GOOD

* Indoors

Supplier Shepards Garden Seeds

Date ordered 1/21/94 #379254 PHONE ($22.+) **Date Received** 2/1 all but # 2/5 + # 2/15

$	#	Name	Quality	Date planted	Performance
1.95	1605	LETTUCE JULIET		3/6	POOR (Soil?)
1.95	1387	BREAD POPPY 'PEPPERBOX'	hold till fall		
1.65	1410	CILANTRO/CORIANDER		4/94	POOR
1.85	965	HELIOTROPE "MARINE"		4/94	GOOD
1.75	920	SWEET PEA 'OLD SPICE'		2/21	ROTTEN
1.85	3430	MOONFLOWER VINE		5/1	"
1.65	1115	* MORNING GLORY BLUE & WHITE		5/1	"
1.55	1000	BORAGE			
1.85	3212	** SUNFLOWER EVENING SUN		5/10	GOOD
1.85	3222	" SUNBEAM . THE VANGOGH		5/10	GOOD
1.75	3217	" ITALIAN WHITE		5/10	GOOD
—	7080	TRIAL GARDENER			

Supplier Heirloom Old Garden Roses

Date ordered 1/9/94 (61.20) Date Received 5/94 After firm phonecall

$	#	Name	Quality	Date planted	Performance
9.95	HM113	GRANDMA'S LACE		5/94	DID Nothing (all alive)
9.95	EN141	L.D. BRAITHWAITE		5/94	DID NOTHING (all alive)
9.95	SH197	QUEEN MARGRETHE	they substituted Gardenia OK	5/94	DID NOTHING (all alive)
9.95	LC869	CL. DAINTY BESS		5/94	wind broke off 12/94
9.95	SI200	WHITE WINGS	on back order	8/94	Worth waiting for!

These roses are 1 year "own root" and are very small

Gardenia had 1 flower before I even got it in the ground

ORDER ACKNOWLEDGED 1/18 CUST ID PHELLI

Supplier WHITE FLOWER FARM

Date ordered 1/22/94 PHONE (41.00) Date Received 3/16/94

$	#	Name	Quality	Date planted	Performance
7.95	32453	IRIS ENSATA 'GOLB BOUND'	OK	3/17	Beautiful
8.95	32486	" 'PINK FROST'	OK	3/17	didn't bloom
18.75	32537	(3) IRIS SIBIRICA 'ORVILLE FAY'	OK	3/17	Great

Supplier Ronnigers Potatoes

Date ordered 2/ /94 Date Received 3/4/94

$	#	Name	Quality	Date planted	Performance
		Caribe	GOOD	3/8	Good
12.75	2	Hansa	↓	3/8	OK
		Yukon Gold		3/8	OK
		German Butterball		3/8	OK
4.00		?GREAT NORTHERNS		5/25	Best!
		WARE'S PRIDE		5/1	Better

SUPPLIERS

Supplier JACKSON & PERKINS TEST GARDEN ROSES

Date ordered ________ Date Received 2/9/94

$	#	Name	Quality	Date planted	Performance
	1837	85-2371 PINK		2/11	Wonderful
	1838	84-926-201 ORG/YEL	SMALLEST OF LOT	2/11	Needs another growing season
	2133	86-5849-018 ORG/WHT		2/11	Yuk
	2175	85-1481 PINK/WHITE	STRONG HEALTHY PLANT	2/11	Fragrant - Nice looked buy

Supplier THOMPSON & MORGAN - Seed order.

Date ordered 2/23 Date Received 3/4

$	#	Name	Quality	Date planted	Performance
2.25		LIBERTIA FORMOSA			
1.65		BALLERINA POPPY	hold til fall	9/94	3 came up!
2.45		HOLLYHOCK SUMMER CARNIVAL			poor
1.85		LUPIN TEXENSIS		5/29	none came up
3.65		COMMELINA DIANTH.			mistake!
1.95		THAI SILK POPPY	SORE SUBJECT! hold til	~~9/94~~ fall	0 came up
.50		TOMATO-SUNGOLD	What a producer!		
2.95		SEAKALE-LILY WHITE			Great

Supplier PARK SEED

Date ordered 3/4/94 Date Received 3/15/94

$	#	Name	Quality	Date planted	Performance
David Austin's New English Rose Collection					
29.95 + 3.95 S&H = $33.94					
Color: Shell Pink	size: 4x4'	Heritage	Poor	3/16	Ready to bloom 5/29
dark crimson	5x5'	Othello	good	3/16	"
white	4x3'	Fair Bianca	OK	3/16	"
Yellow	8x5'	Graham Thomas	Very vigorous	3/16*	Just starting to grow
rich pink	4x4'	Mary Rose	OK	3/16	Ready to Bloom 5/29

* Called & said that this rose didn't appear to be alive 5/1 They reshipped the new one looked sad & hasn't started growth yet 5/29

Supplier Heronswood Nursery Kingston Wa

Date ordered Feb Date Received 3/2/95

$	#	Name	Quality	Date planted	Performance
4.00	1	Salvia puberula	helper at nursery broke off part	3/17	(Pink?)
6.00	1	Nepeta Blue Beauty	ok	3/17	
15.00	3	Nepeta x faassenii Pool Bank	ok		
10.00	1	Hydrangea "Goliath"	good		
10.00	1	Corydallis "Pere David"	good		
8.00	1	Philadelphus Bouquet Blanc	Small		
5.00	1	Angelica Gigas	OK		
8.00	1	Miscanthus sinensis Purpurascens	good		

Supplier Kingston Garden Shop

Date ordered Date Received 3/2/95

$	#	Name	Quality	Date planted	Performance
	7	Veronica Sunny Border Blue	Good	5 3/17	
	3	Primrose			
	2	Primrose Candleabra			

Supplier Skyline Nursery

Date ordered Date Received 3/11/95

$	#	Name	Quality	Date planted	Performance
6.00		Japanese Iris	good		
5.00		Lavatera "Candy Floss"	great		
5.25		Helianthemum	good		
5.00		Hebe	great		

SUPPLIERS

Supplier ______

Date ordered ______ Date Received ______

$	#	Name	Quality	Date planted	Performance

Supplier ______

Date ordered ______ Date Received ______

$	#	Name	Quality	Date planted	Performance

Supplier ______

Date ordered ______ Date Received ______

$	#	Name	Quality	Date planted	Performance

Supplier ______________________

Date ordered ______________ Date Received ______________

$	#	Name	Quality	Date planted	Performance

Supplier ______________________

Date ordered ______________ Date Received ______________

$	#	Name	Quality	Date planted	Performance

Supplier ______________________

Date ordered ______________ Date Received ______________

$	#	Name	Quality	Date planted	Performance

SUPPLIERS

Supplier ______________________________

Date ordered ______________ Date Received ______________

$	#	Name	Quality	Date planted	Performance

Supplier ______________________________

Date ordered ______________ Date Received ______________

$	#	Name	Quality	Date planted	Performance

Supplier ______________________________

Date ordered ______________ Date Received ______________

$	#	Name	Quality	Date planted	Performance

Supplier ____________________

Date ordered ____________________ Date Received ____________________

$	#	Name	Quality	Date planted	Performance

Supplier ____________________

Date ordered ____________________ Date Received ____________________

$	#	Name	Quality	Date planted	Performance

Supplier ____________________

Date ordered ____________________ Date Received ____________________

$	#	Name	Quality	Date planted	Performance

NAMES AND ADDRESSES

Plant societies, garden clubs, public gardens

Name
Address
State/Zip
Phone
Dues

Name
Address
State/Zip
Phone
Dues

Name
Address
State/Zip
Phone
Dues

Name
Address
State/Zip
Phone
Dues

Name
Address
State/Zip
Phone
Dues

Name
Address
State/Zip
Phone
Dues

Name
Address
State/Zip
Phone
Dues

Name
Address
State/Zip
Phone
Dues

Name
Address
State/Zip
Phone
Dues

Name
Address
State/Zip
Phone
Dues

Name
Address
State/Zip
Phone
Dues

Name
Address
State/Zip
Phone
Dues

Name
Address
State/Zip
Phone
Dues

Name
Address
State/Zip
Phone
Dues

Publications, horticultural libraries, bookstores

Name
Address
State/Zip
Phone
Subscription

Name
Address
State/Zip
Phone
Subscription

Name
Address
State/Zip
Phone
Subscription

Name
Address
State/Zip
Phone
Subscription

Name
Address
State/Zip
Phone
Subscription

Name
Address
State/Zip
Phone
Subscription

Name
Address
State/Zip
Phone
Subscription

Name
Address
State/Zip
Phone
Subscription

Name
Address
State/Zip
Phone
Subscription

Name
Address
State/Zip
Phone
Subscription

Name
Address
State/Zip
Phone
Subscription

Name
Address
State/Zip
Phone
Subscription

Name
Address
State/Zip
Phone
Subscription

Name
Address
State/Zip
Phone
Subscription

NAMES AND ADDRESSES

Name
Address
State/Zip
Phone

Name
Address
State/Zip
Phone

Name
Address
State/Zip
Phone

Name
Address
State/Zip
Phone

Name
Address
State/Zip
Phone

Name
Address
State/Zip
Phone

Name
Address
State/Zip
Phone

Name
Address
State/Zip
Phone

Name
Address
State/Zip
Phone

Name
Address
State/Zip
Phone

Name
Address
State/Zip
Phone

Name
Address
State/Zip
Phone

Name
Address
State/Zip
Phone

Name
Address
State/Zip
Phone

Name
Address
State/Zip
Phone

Name
Address
State/Zip
Phone

Name
Address
State/Zip
Phone

Name
Address
State/Zip
Phone